meatless EASY-OVEN *cookbook*

MENU PLANNING MADE SIMPLE
WITH VEGETARIAN RECIPES THAT LET YOU
BAKE A WHOLE MEAL
AT THE SAME TIME

Debi AND Jim Pedersen

Pacific Press® Publishing Association
Nampa, Idaho
Oshawa, Ontario, Canada

www.PacificPress.com

Designed by Michelle C. Petz
Cover illustration by Mike Cressy

Additional copies of this book are available by calling toll free 1.800.765.6955 or visiting AdventistBookCenter.com

Library of Congress Cataloging-in-Publication Data:

Pedersen, Debi, 1956-
Meatless easy-oven cookbook : menu planning made simple with vegetarian recipes that let you bake a whole meal at the same time / Debi and Jim Pedersen.
p. cm.
ISBN 0-8163-1969-3
1. Vegetarian cookery. I. Pedersen, Jim, 1952- II. Title

TX837.P43 2003
641.5'636–dc21

2002192580

03 04 05 06 07 • 5 4 3 2 1

Contents

Dedication

This book is lovingly dedicated to the memory of

Patricia Rose,

Debi's mother, who was
an inspiration in the kitchen
and

LeRoy Pedersen,

Jim's father, who was employed at Pacific Press
for twenty-seven years.

Acknowledgments

Our thanks go first to our daughter Lisa for her help in so many ways to make this book a reality. She baked off our creations each evening for supper, gave us her honest opinions, and endured many "baked" meals when what she really wanted was tacos!

To our family, friends, co-workers, and teachers who tasted our creations and gave their honest opinions. And to those who shared their ideas and recipes.

To Matthew Kates and the Worthington® Foods division of the Kellogg® Company for the generosity and support shown in the writing of this book.

To James T. Ehler—webmaster, cook, chef, writer—for his graciousness in allowing the use of food history and trivia facts found on his Web site **www.foodreference.com.**

Introduction

Nowdays, our lives are busier than ever before. We want to make nice meals for our family and friends, but we don't have time to search for and organize recipes into menus. That's where this book can help! Tasty recipes are grouped by oven temperature so that both our personal energy and our ovens' energy can be used efficiently.

This book is arranged to be convenient and easy to use for meal planning. Begin by choosing an entree from one of the first three chapters, and follow with a side dish from the same chapter. Then move on to chapter 4 ("Make-Ahead Dishes") and chapter 5 ("Make-at-the-Last-Minute Dishes") to complete the meal with salads, sides, breads, gravies/sauces, and desserts. We have used this method for years, and it helps us to be able to visit with our guests and reduce before-meal stress!

A number of recipes use canned or frozen meat analogs manufactured under the names of Loma Linda®, Morningstar Farms®, Natural Touch®, and Worthington®—all owned by the Kellogg® Company. These can be obtained from many supermarkets and health food stores.

Now, some tips on how to "read" this cookbook. Each recipe has these assumptions:

- Baked recipes assume the oven has been preheated.
- "Greased" means with nonstick cooking spray, unless otherwise noted.
- All dishes are baked uncovered unless stated otherwise; "covered" generally means with foil.
- A dish specified by quart size refers to a deep, round dish.
- "Number of servings" includes one serving per person without seconds.

Here are some helpful hints when baking your meals:

- Oven temperatures vary, so test yours with a reliable oven thermometer.
- If you're putting a glass dish in the oven directly from the refrigerator, it's a good idea to put it in a cold oven and heat it with the oven. This will prevent cracking the dish! Adjust baking time as needed.
- Dishes not at room temperature when baked may need a longer baking time.
- The more items in the oven at the same time, the more likely the baking time will need to be increased.

- As much as possible, bake dishes in the center of the oven. If multiple items are being baked at the same time, leave airflow space around each dish, including space between them and the oven walls.
- Depending on how even or uneven your oven bakes, if you are baking more than one item on multiple shelves, the dishes may need to be rotated to assure even baking. This means both from side to side and top to bottom.
- Some recipes need no extra attention when being baked; others need removal of foil, etc. Keep this in mind when choosing your menu to match your needs.
- If you wish to use the "time bake" feature on your oven while you're away, choose recipes that bake at the same temperature for the same amount of time.

We hope this book will inspire you to use your oven as a starting point for meal planning. It has been a joy for us to create this collection of recipes for you. Bon appétit!

We've chosen a variety of recipes that can be combined in many different ways to create special meals for all occasions. Here is a sampling of menus to get you going.

Summer Faire *(350 Degrees)*

Numete Cashew Loaf (Ch. 1)
with Tomato Gravy (Ch. 5)
Lemon-Herb Potato Puff (Ch. 1)
Fresh Mozzarella and Tomato Salad (Ch. 5)
Green-Bean Bundles (Ch. 5)
Strawberry Shortcake Trifle (Ch. 4)

Flavors of Mexico *(375 Degrees)*

Mexican Casserole With Spinach (Ch. 2)
Chile Cheese Rice Casserole (Ch. 2)
Confetti Salad (Ch. 5)
Salsa Muffins (Ch. 5)
Dulce de Leche Cheesecake (Ch. 4)

Casual Lunch *(400 Degrees)*

Baked Reuben Sandwich (Ch. 3)
Parmesan Potato Wedges (Ch. 3)
Asparagus, Apples, Chicken Salad (Ch. 5)
Mango Salad (Ch. 4)
Cherry Brown Betty (Ch. 4)

Throughout the book, an asterisk (*) refers to those food facts found at ***www.foodreference.com.*** *Used by permission of James T. Ehler. This Web site is a wonderful resource for cooking tips, articles, recipes, shopping, and other food-related interests.*

*(**Note:** Nutritional analysis was calculated with the Master Cook® software program. Results may vary depending on product used for the calculation.)*

Chapter 1: 350 Degrees

Entrees

Side Dishes

Artichoke Chicken Strudel

Even though artichokes have been around for centuries, they were "rediscovered" in 1922 by Andrew Molera, who turned his California sugar-beet fields over to this "new" vegetable.

1 medium onion, finely chopped
2 cloves garlic, minced
3/4 cup butter, divided
3 6-ounce jars marinated artichoke hearts, drained, chopped
1/3 cup grated Parmesan cheese
1 13-ounce can Worthington® Meatless Chicken Diced, drained
1 8-ounce package fat-free cream cheese, softened
1 cup low-fat cottage cheese
3 eggs or 3/4 cup Morningstar Farms® *Scramblers®*
1/2 cup cracker meal
1 teaspoon marjoram
1 teaspoon parsley
3/4 teaspoon tarragon
1 teaspoon garlic salt
1 16-ounce package (20 sheets) phyllo dough, thawed

Sauté onion and garlic in 1/4 cup butter. Mix together all ingredients except phyllo sheets and 1/2 cup butter.

Melt 1/2 cup butter. Using one-third of phyllo sheets, begin by laying out 1 sheet; spread it thoroughly with melted butter. Add second sheet, third, etc., up to eight, buttering between each layer.

Place one-third of filling in log-type roll at bottom of sheets. Tuck in sides and roll jellyroll fashion. Butter top and sides of completed roll. Continue with other sheets, forming 3 rolls. Place rolls on greased baking sheet(s). Bake for 30 to 45 minutes. Cut each roll into 8 pieces.

Note: *Bake only what you need and freeze the rest for future use.*

Makes 12 servings. Per serving: *358 Calories; 17g Fat; 15g Protein; 35g Carbohydrate; 90mg Cholesterol; 782mg Sodium*

Chicken Cups

For those of you who like the "crunchy" on the outside edges of a roast, you'll love these individual casseroles in a cup.

1 pound Worthington® *Chic-ketts®*, thawed, ground
1/4 cup finely chopped celery
1/3 cup chopped fresh parsley
3 cloves garlic, minced
2 teaspoons onion powder
1 tablespoon brewer's yeast flakes
1 teaspoon salt
1 teaspoon soy sauce
1 1/2 cups cooked rice
1/4 cup Kellogg's® Corn Flake Crumbs
1 tablespoon chickenlike seasoning and broth mix
1/2 cup Parmesan cheese
4 eggs, slightly beaten, or
1 cup Morningstar Farms® *Scramblers®*
1 1/2 cups low-fat cottage cheese
1/2 cup buttermilk
1/2 cup slivered almonds, chopped

In a large mixing bowl, combine all ingredients except the almonds. Divide filling among 16 greased muffin cups. Sprinkle with diced almonds. Bake for 40 to 45 minutes or until set. Serve with White Sauce (see p. 155) or Chicken Gravy (see p. 152).

Makes 8 servings. Per serving: *341 Calories; 17g Fat; 28g Protein; 20g Carbohydrate; 114mg Cholesterol; 1217mg Sodium*

Crunchy Skallops Casserole

Jim created this recipe when he was in high school! It became a "regular" in their home.

- 1 20-ounce can Worthington® *Vegetable Skallops®*
- 1 8-ounce can sliced water chestnuts, chopped
- 1/2 cup chopped celery
- 1/2 cup slivered almonds
- 1 cup light mayonnaise
- 1 teaspoon onion powder
- 2 packets G. Washington's® Golden Seasoning and Broth
- 2 cloves garlic, minced
- 2 tablespoons flour
- 3/4 cup water
- 2 eggs or 1/2 cup Morningstar Farms® *Scramblers®*
- 2 cups chow mein noodles

Cut *Skallops®* into smaller pieces as desired; place in a large mixing bowl. Add water chestnuts, celery, and almonds.

In a separate bowl, whisk together the mayonnaise, seasonings, flour, water, and eggs. Pour egg mixture into *Skallops®* and stir. Fold in chow mein noodles. Pour into a greased 7" x 11" baking dish. Cover and bake for 45 minutes, removing foil the last 15 minutes.

Makes 8 servings. Per serving: *226 Calories; 12g Fat; 13g Protein; 18g Carbohydrate; 66mg Cholesterol; 695mg Sodium*

Harvest Meatballs With Sauce

BY MARTHA PAPPAS

Soon after we were married, we went to visit Debi's aunt and uncle. Aunt Martha had not cooked vegetarian before, and she searched for an entree to make for us. It was great! We like these meatballs because they are baked, not fried.

- 1 cup cooked brown rice
- 1 cup ground peanuts
- 2 cups shredded Swiss cheese
- 1 egg
- 1/2 cup minced onions or 2 tablespoons onion powder, divided
- 1/4 teaspoon rosemary
- 1/4 teaspoon thyme
- 1 tablespoon oil
- 1 clove garlic, crushed
- 1 14.5-ounce can diced tomatoes
- 1/4 cup finely chopped dill pickles
- 1/2 teaspoon salt
- 1 teaspoon cornstarch
- 2 teaspoons water

Mix rice, peanuts, cheese, egg, 1/4 cup onion, herbs, and garlic well. Press firmly into walnut-size balls. Place in a greased 8" x 8" baking dish. Cover and bake for 20 to 25 minutes.

Meanwhile, in a medium saucepan, make sauce by sautéing garlic in oil until tender. Stir in tomatoes, dill pickle, 1/4 cup onion, and salt.

Blend cornstarch into cold water; stir into tomato mixture. Heat to boiling, stirring constantly. Boil 2 minutes. Pour hot sauce over baked meatballs and serve.

Makes 6 servings. Per serving: *371 Calories; 26g Fat; 20g Protein; 18g Carbohydrate; 70mg Cholesterol; 613mg Sodium*

Mexicali Chicken Bake

Did you know that an ear of corn always has an even number of rows because of the genetic formula that divides the cells? The average ear of corn has 800 kernels, arranged in 16 rows.* The corn in this casserole brings a sweetness and familiar flavor.

350°

1 12.5-ounce can Worthington® *Low Fat FriChik®*, torn in small pieces
1/4 cup finely chopped onion
or 1 teaspoon onion powder
1 4-ounce can diced green chiles, drained
2 cups shredded low-fat Monterey Jack cheese
1 11-ounce can Mexican-style corn, drained
1 cup biscuit mix
1 cup 2% milk
1/2 teaspoon salt
3 eggs, separated

In a greased 7" x 11" baking dish, layer chicken, onion, chiles, cheese, and corn.

Beat together biscuit mix, milk, salt, and egg yolks.

Beat egg whites in large bowl until stiff; fold into biscuit mixture. Pour over corn. Bake until knife inserted in center comes out clean, about 35 to 40 minutes.

Note: *If you're short on time and energy, mix in the whole egg and omit beating the white. The result will still be good, just not quite as puffy.*

Makes 6 servings. Per serving: *347 Calories; 16g Fat; 20g Protein; 29g Carbohydrate; 376mg Cholesterol; 1154mg Sodium*

Mexican Tofu Casserole

BY MELISSA KRAUSE

Melissa and Nathan, a pastoral couple who are friends of ours, eat vegan. They gave us a wonderful tofu recipe that's very easy to prepare.

- 2 tablespoons olive oil
- 1 medium onion, finely chopped, or 2 teaspoons onion powder
- 3 12.3-ounce packages firm, low-fat tofu, drained
- 1 1/2 tablespoons chickenlike seasoning and broth mix
- 2 teaspoons cumin
- 1 teaspoon turmeric
- 1 4-ounce can diced green chiles, drained
- 1 3.8-ounce can sliced olives, drained
- 2 16-ounce cans tomato sauce
- 2 cups tortilla chips
- 1 cup shredded low-fat cheddar cheese

Sauté onion in olive oil until tender. Crumble in tofu. Add seasonings and blend well. Add chiles and olives.

Pour one-third of the tomato sauce into a greased 9" x 13" casserole dish. Crumble one-third of the chips on top of sauce. Next, layer one third of the tofu mixture. Make 2 more layers of the sauce, chips, and tofu mixture. Top with shredded cheese. Bake for 35 minutes.

Makes 8 servings. Per serving: *259 Calories; 11g Fat; 13g Protein; 22g Carbohydrate; 3mg Cholesterol; 1303mg Sodium*

Numete Cashew Loaf

Nuts are one of the vegetarian's main sources of protein. This combination of peanuts (in the *Numete®)* and cashews is high in protein. Also, leftovers make a tasty sandwich filling.

350°

- 1 tablespoon oil
- 1 1/2 cups chopped mushrooms (about 6 medium)
- 1 stalk celery, finely chopped
- 1/2 medium onion, finely chopped, or 2 teaspoons onion powder
- 1 19-ounce can Worthington® *Numete®*, grated, or Loma Linda® *Nuteena®*
- 1/2 cup chopped cashews
- 1/4 cup chopped fresh parsley or 1 tablespoon dried parsley
- 1 1/2 teaspoons dried basil
- 1 1/2 teaspoons brewer's yeast
- 3 eggs or 3/4 cup Morningstar Farms® *Scramblers®*
- 1/3 cup hot water
- 2 teaspoons Savorex® yeast paste

Sauté mushrooms, celery, and onion in oil until soft.

In large mixing bowl combine *Numete®*, cashews, seasonings, and eggs. Add sautéed vegetables.

Dissolve Savorex® in hot water and stir into *Numete®* mixture, mixing well.

Grease a loaf pan well; in the bottom only place a piece of greased waxed paper or parchment. Spread mixture evenly in the pan. Cover and bake for 60 minutes, removing covering during the last 15 minutes. Loosen sides of roast with knife and invert onto serving plate. Remove paper and slice. Serve with a favorite gravy.

Makes 8 servings. Per serving: *262 Calories; 20g Fat; 72g Protein; 10g Carbohydrate; 80mg Cholesterol; 480mg Sodium*

Savory Chicken Cheesecake

Jim is known for making cheesecake desserts. So when he became a finalist in the "Taste of Goodness" contest, the first thing our friends jokingly said was, "What did you do—make a *FriChik®* cheesecake?" Well . . . that gave us an idea!

- 36 butter flavor crackers
- 1/4 cup butter, melted
- 1/4 cup finely chopped pecans
- 1/4 cup grated Parmesan cheese
- 1 tablespoon olive oil
- 2 cloves garlic, crushed
- 1/2 cup crumbled feta cheese
- 2 8-ounce packages fat-free cream cheese, room temperature
- 1/2 cup part-skim-milk ricotta cheese
- 2 tablespoons flour
- 3 eggs or 3/4 cup Morningstar Farms® *Scramblers®*
- 1/4 cup evaporated skim milk
- 1 teaspoon onion powder
- 1/4 teaspoon crushed oregano
- 1/4 teaspoon crushed thyme
- 1/4 teaspoon crushed basil
- 1/4 teaspoon crushed marjoram
- 1/2 teaspoon chickenlike seasoning and broth mix
- 1/2 pound Worthington® *Chic-ketts®*, coarsely grated

CRUST: Combine crackers, butter, pecans, and Parmesan cheese in food processor; pulse until finely blended. Butter the sides of a 9" springform pan; coat the sides of the pan with some of the cracker mixture; press the remaining crumbs into the bottom of the pan. Place pan in the freezer while the filling is prepared.

FILLING: Sauté the garlic in the olive oil over low heat (do not allow to brown); let cool. Press the feta through a medium sieve. In bowl of electric mixer, blend feta, cream cheese, and ricotta until smooth; add flour. Add eggs one at a time, beating well after each addition. Slowly add evaporated milk. Mix in herbs, chickenlike seasoning, and garlic just until well blended. Remove bowl from mixer. By hand, fold in chicken pieces just until blended. Pour filling mixture into prepared crust. Bake for 60 minutes, checking carefully after 45 minutes. Cheesecake should be set in the middle, golden brown on the top. Allow to set 10 minutes before serving.

Makes 8 servings. Per serving: *385 Calories; 23g Fat; 23g Protein; 22g Carbohydrate; 118mg Cholesterol; 869mg Sodium*

Sweet-and-Sour Nut Balls

These "meatballs" are a holiday or special occasion standby. We've served them to nonvegetarians who loved them and didn't realize they were meatless.

- 5 eggs or 1 1/4 cups Morningstar Farms® *Scramblers®*
- 1 cup shredded low-fat cheddar cheese
- 1/2 cup low-fat cottage cheese
- 1/2 cup finely chopped onion
- 1 cup finely chopped walnuts
- 1 teaspoon basil
- 1 1/2 teaspoon salt, divided
- 1/2 teaspoon sage
- 2 cups crushed herb-seasoned stuffing
- 1/4 cup oil
- 1/2 cup vinegar
- 1 cup apricot jam
- 1 cup ketchup
- 1 teaspoon onion powder
- 1 teaspoon oregano

Mix eggs, cheese, cottage cheese, onion, walnuts, basil, 1/2 teaspoon salt, sage, and stuffing; form into walnut-size balls. Place balls in a greased 9" x 13" baking dish. Combine remaining ingredients; pour over nut balls. Bake for 35 to 40 minutes.

Makes 8 servings. Per serving: *498 Calories; 21g Fat; 18g Protein; 60g Carbohydrate; 137mg Cholesterol; 1751mg Sodium*

Swiss Steak

BY PATRICIA ROSE

Certain dishes and flavors take us back to our childhoods. Swiss Steak has always been a favorite in Debi's family, and so she adapted the recipe for vegetarians.

- 1 20-ounce can Worthington® *Choplets®*, drained, or Worthington® *Multi-Grain Cutlets®*
- 1 14.5-ounce can stewed tomatoes, crushed
- 1 medium onion, finely chopped, or 1 tablespoon dried minced onion
- 1/2 teaspoon salt
- 1 teaspoon crushed dried oregano
- 1/2 teaspoon garlic powder
- 1/4 teaspoon sugar
- 1 tablespoon beeflike seasoning and broth mix
- 2 tablespoons vegetable oil
- 2 tablespoons flour
- Water (enough to cover steaks)

Cut *Choplets®* into quarters. Combine with remaining ingredients in a 2-quart baking dish. Cover and bake for 60 to 75 minutes. Serve over mashed potatoes.

Makes 6 servings. Per serving: *140 Calories; 6g Fat; 12g Protein; l0g Carbohydrate; 0mg Cholesterol; 1009mg Sodium*

350°

Tortilla Flats Casserole

We used to fill the tortillas and roll them like enchiladas. But since "quicker is better" these days, we have switched to layering the ingredients instead.

350°

- 24 corn tortillas, cut into 1" squares
- 1 2.25-ounce can sliced black olives, drained
- 1 small onion, chopped, or 1 tablespoon onion powder
- 4 cups shredded low-fat Monterey Jack cheese
- 1/4 cup butter
- 1/4 cup flour
- 2 cups water
- 2 teaspoons Vegex® yeast paste
- 1 cup light sour cream
- 1 4-ounce can diced green chiles

Grease a 9" x 13" baking dish. Layer half of each: tortillas, olives, and onions; sprinkle on 1 1/2 cups cheese. Repeat layers.

Make sauce by melting butter in 1 1/2 quart saucepan. Stir in flour until well mixed. Add water and Vegex®; boil the mixture until thickened. Remove from heat; add sour cream and mix until creamy. Add diced chiles. Pour sauce over tortillas. Top with 1 cup cheese. Bake for 20 to 25 minutes or until bubbly.

Makes 8 servings. Per serving: *460 Calories; 21g Fat; 18g Protein; 44g Carbohydrate; 418mg Cholesterol; 799mg Sodium*

Turkey Spinach Pie

This is our version of a vegetarian turkey dish we once had at a restaurant in Redlands, California. We like to copy dishes we've eaten in restaurants that we find especially delicious.

2 8-ounce packages refrigerated crescent rolls
6 eggs or 1 1/2 cups Morningstar Farms® *Scramblers®*
1 quart low-fat cottage cheese
1/4 cup flour
1/2 cup buttermilk
1/4 cup butter, melted
1/2 teaspoon salt
1 teaspoon onion powder
1 teaspoon garlic powder
2 10-ounce packages frozen chopped spinach, thawed and drained
1 8-ounce package Worthington® Meatless Smoked Turkey Slices, thawed
1 cup grated Parmesan cheese

In a greased 9" x 13" baking dish, line bottom and sides with 1 1/2 packages of unrolled crescents, pressing edges together to seal.

In a large mixing bowl, beat eggs; add rest of ingredients except turkey and Parmesan cheese. Mix well. Spread half of spinach mixture over crescents. Cover with turkey slices; top with rest of the spinach mixture. Sprinkle the top with Parmesan cheese. Roll the last 1/4 of the crescent rolls into a rectangle. Cut into 1/2" strips and weave diagonally into a lattice, leaving one-inch spaces between rows. Bake for 45 minutes or until set.

Makes 12 servings. Per serving: *375 Calories; 19g Fat; 48g Protein; 25g Carbohydrate; 128mg Cholesterol; 1148mg Sodium*

Vegeburger "Boats"

One day Jim's mind was wandering—and this was the result.
Our nonvegetarian neighbors thought these tasted like "more!"

10 medium (5 inches long) baking potatoes
1/4 cup margarine
3 cloves garlic, minced
6 slices wheat bread, crust trimmed, cubed
1 19-ounce can Worthington® Low Fat Vegetarian Burger
4 eggs or 1 cup Morningstar Farms® *Scramblers®*
2 cups shredded low-fat cheddar cheese
1/2 teaspoon sage
1 1/2 teaspoons onion powder
1 teaspoon beeflike seasoning and broth mix

Bake the potatoes in foil until just barely done (350°F for 75 to 90 minutes). Allow to cool; remove foil. Slice off the top of the potatoes (lengthwise); scoop out the insides, leaving a solid shell about 1/8" thick. (Use the scooped-out potato pulp for Refrigerator Mashed Potatoes—see p. 38—or in soup, etc.) Set "boats" in greased 10" x 15" baking dish or baking sheet.

Sauté garlic and bread in margarine.

In large mixing bowl combine burger, eggs, cheese, and seasonings; add bread mixture. Mix thoroughly. Allow to rest for 10 minutes. Spoon into potato skin "boats." Top with additional shredded cheese, if desired. Cover and bake for 45 minutes, removing foil the last 15 minutes. Serve with favorite gravy.

Note: *"Wendy's Loaf" (see p. 23) may be used as the filling for these "boats"; however, it will need 2 more potatoes.*

Makes 10 servings. Per serving: *344 Calories; 10g Fat; 22g Protein; 37g Carbohydrate; 90mg Cholesterol; 625mg Sodium*

Vegetable Lasagna

Years ago, when the frozen vegetable lasagna first came out, we decided to create our own version—and here it is!

1/4 cup + 3 tablespoons margarine, divided
3 tablespoons flour
3 cups 2% milk
1 3/4 cups grated Parmesan cheese, divided
12 lasagna noodles, cooked and drained
3 cups part-skim-milk ricotta cheese
4 large carrots, peeled and shredded
2 10-ounce packages frozen chopped spinach, thawed and drained dry
2 teaspoons garlic powder
4 cups part-skim-milk shredded mozzarella
1 cup bread crumbs

In medium saucepan melt 3 tablespoons margarine; remove from heat. Stir in flour until well mixed. Return pan to heat and gradually add the milk, stirring and heating until thick. Add 1 cup Parmesan cheese.

Cover the bottom of a greased 9" x 13" baking dish with a small amount of cheese sauce. Place 4 lasagna noodles over sauce. Layer with half of each: ricotta cheese, carrots, spinach, garlic powder, and sauce; sprinkle with one-third of the mozzarella. Add 4 more lasagna noodles and repeat the layering, ending with 4 noodles and mozzarella cheese on top.

Melt 1/4 cup margarine. Add bread crumbs and 3/4 cup Parmesan cheese, mixing thoroughly. Spread evenly over top. Bake for 30 to 45 minutes, allowing to cool 10 minutes before serving.

Makes 12 servings. Per serving: *493 Calories; 23g Fat; 31g Protein; 42g Carbohydrate; 53mg Cholesterol; 694mg Sodium*

Vegetarian Chicken Kiev

Wondering if it would work to stuff *FriChik®*, Debi tried it, and this creation turned out to be a winner. Originally, the dish came, not from Russia as the name might suggest, but from New York, developed by a chef trying to please the many new Russian immigrants.

- 1 42-ounce can Worthington® *Low Fat FriChik®*, drained
- 1/4 cup butter, room temperature
- 1/4 cup finely chopped fresh basil
- 1/2 cup grated fresh Parmesan cheese
- 3 cloves garlic, minced
- 1/3 cup flour
- 1/2 teaspoon salt
- 2 egg whites or 1/2 cup Egg Beaters® Egg Whites
- 2 tablespoons water
- 3/4 cup bread crumbs

Squeeze moisture from each piece of *FriChik®*. Slice into the center of each piece, making a deep pocket but taking care not to cut all the way through.

Mix butter, basil, cheese, and garlic. Fill each piece of *FriChik®* with the mixture and press closed to seal. Be sure to use all the filling.

In a small bowl combine flour and salt.

In a separate bowl, wisk together egg whites and water.

Place bread crumbs in third bowl.

Dredge each piece of chicken in flour, then dip in the egg-white mixture, and finally coat with bread crumbs. Place chicken on greased baking sheet. Bake for 20 to 30 minutes until heated through, turning after 10 minutes.

Makes 8 serving. Per serving: *220 Calories; 11g Fat; 15g Protein; 14g Carbohydrate; 19mg Cholesterol; 799mg Sodium*

Wendy's Loaf

BY JEANNE PEDERSEN

Jim's mother has made this roast for many years, and now it's also a favorite of our daughters, Stacey and Lisa. It uses walnuts, which were thought in medieval times to cure headaches!

- 6 eggs or 11/2 cups Morningstar Farms® *Scramblers®*
- 1 quart low-fat cottage cheese
- 1/2 cup margarine, softened
- 1 cup chopped walnuts
- 1 envelope onion soup mix
- 6 cups Kellogg's® *Special K®* cereal

Mix all ingredients in large mixing bowl. Put into greased 9" x 13" baking dish. Cover and bake for 75 minutes, removing cover the final 15 minutes.

Note: *This loaf can also be used as the filling for the "Vegeburger 'Boats'" (see p. 20). However, it will need two more potato "boats."*

Makes 12 servings. Per serving: *286 Calories; 16g Fat; 20g Protein; 17g Carbohydrate; 113mg Cholesterol; 812mg Sodium*

Apricot Barley Casserole

Barley is one of the world's oldest domesticated grains. In Rome, barley was the special food of the gladiators. It was also used as currency and as a measuring standard.* Here, apricots add a wonderful sweetness and balance, and the dish is a nice alternative to rice or potatoes. It makes a wonderful "autumn" dish.

- 4 tablespoons butter, divided
- 2/3 cup slivered almonds or pine nuts
- 2 cups pearl barley
- 7 cups vegetable broth or 7 cups water with 7 teaspoons chickenstyle seasoning and broth mix
- 2 teaspoons onion powder
- 1 cup diced dried apricots
- 1/2 cup dried cranberries
- 1/2 cup finely chopped parsley

In a skillet, sauté nuts in 1 tablespoon butter until lightly browned; remove and set aside.

In the same skillet, sauté the barley in remaining butter until golden. Add broth and onion powder; bring to a boil. Stir in the apricots, cranberries, parsley, and nuts. Pour into a greased 9" x 13" baking dish. Bake for 60 minutes or until barley is tender.

Note: *If making ahead and refrigerating overnight, add nuts and stir just before baking.*

Makes 12 servings. Per serving: *240 Calories; 9g Fat; 6g Protein; 36g Carbohydrate; 10mg Cholesterol; 612mg Sodium*

Broccoli Risotto Torte

Arborio rice is a special short-grain rice that, because of its extra starch, adds a creamy texture to recipes. A few steps are needed to prepare this torte, but the result is elegant and delicious.

- 8 ounces broccoli florets, cut small
- 2 tablespoons olive oil
- 1/4 cup butter
- 1 small onion, finely chopped
- 2 cloves garlic, minced
- 1 large yellow bell pepper, halved, sliced thin
- 1 1/4 cups arborio rice
- 1/2 cup white grape juice
- 4 1/2 cups vegetable broth
- 1/2 teaspoon salt
- 1/2 cup grated Parmesan cheese
- 4 eggs, separated

Heat water to boiling in a small saucepan. Blanch the broccoli in the water for 3 minutes; then drain and set aside.

In a large saucepan, gently fry the onion, garlic, and pepper in the oil and butter for 5 minutes until they are soft. Stir in the rice, cook for a minute, then pour in the juice. Cook, stirring, until the liquid is absorbed. Pour in the broth, season with salt, bring to a boil, then lower to a simmer. Cook for 20 minutes, stirring occasionally.

Meanwhile, grease and line with waxed paper a deep 10" round cake pan. A greased 10" springform pan may also be used.

Stir the cheese and broccoli into the rice, allow the mixture to cool for 5 minutes, then beat in the egg yolks.

Whisk the egg whites until they form soft peaks and carefully fold into the rice. Turn into the prepared pan. Bake for 60 to 75 minutes until risen, golden brown, and set in the center. Let set 10 minutes; then run a knife around the edge of the pan and shake out onto a serving plate, removing the wax paper before serving.

Makes 8 servings. Per serving: *284 Calories; 14g Fat; 9g Protein; 31g Carbohydrate; 126mg Cholesterol; 941mg Sodium*

Cheesy Barbecued Potatoes

The Irish have a saying, "Only two things in this world are too serious to be jested on, potatoes and matrimony."* We're not jesting with this different-from-the-usual style for potatoes. The sauce is smooth and savory.

350°

4 cups shredded sharp cheddar cheese
2 cans condensed cream of mushroom soup
2/3 cup 2% milk
1/4 cup barbecue sauce
1/2 teaspoon oregano
1/2 teaspoon salt
8 medium potatoes, cooked, sliced thin
1 teaspoon paprika

Combine 3 cups cheese, soup, milk, barbecue sauce, oregano, and salt; mix well. Stir in potatoes. Pour mixture into greased 9" x 13" baking dish. Cover and bake for 60 minutes, removing foil the last 15 minutes. Sprinkle with remaining cheese and paprika.

Makes 12 servings. Per serving: *274 Calories; 17g Fat; 12g Protein; 19g Carbohydrate; 41mg Cholesterol; 788mg Sodium*

Chile Relleno Casserole

BY DAWN HASHEMI

Debi's friend Dawn gave her this recipe years ago. It's a great make-ahead casserole.

- 1 7-ounce can whole green chiles, halved and seeded
- 2 cups shredded low-fat Monterey Jack cheese
- 2 cups shredded low-fat cheddar cheese
- 1 small onion, finely chopped
- 1/2 teaspoon garlic powder
- 1/2 teaspoon salt
- 10 eggs, beaten
- 2 cups evaporated skim milk
- 1/3 cup (heaping) flour
- 1 tablespoon baking powder

350°

In a greased 9" x 13" baking dish, layer half of each: chiles, cheeses, onion, garlic powder, and salt. Repeat the layers.

Mix together eggs, milk, flour, and baking powder. Pour over chile-cheese layers. Let stand overnight in the refrigerator. Bake for 60 to 75 minutes or until set.

Makes 12 servings. Per serving: *222 Calories; 10g Fat; 18g Protein; 11g Carbohydrate; 316mg Cholesterol; 603mg Sodium*

Grandpa's Thanksgiving Yams

BY RICHARD ROSE

Despite a physical similarity and a frequent confusion with their names, yams and sweet potatoes are not even distantly related. They are in two different botanical families. Yams are actually related to grasses and lilies.* Debi's dad makes this yummy yam (or are they sweet potatoes?) recipe, which has become a Thanksgiving tradition in his home.

350°

- 1 29-ounce can yams, drained, mashed
- 1/4 cup + 3 tablespoons butter, melted, divided
- 1 teaspoon vanilla
- 1/4 cup granulated sugar
- 2 eggs or 1/2 cup Morningstar Farms® *Scramblers*®
- 1/2 teaspoon salt
- 1/3 cup flour
- 1 teaspoon cinnamon
- 1 teaspoon allspice
- 1/2 cup brown sugar, packed
- 1/2 cup pecans, whole or pieces

Mix together yams, 1/4 cup butter, vanilla, granulated sugar, eggs, salt, flour, cinnamon, and allspice. Beat with an electric hand mixer until fluffy and pour into a greased 1 1/2-quart baking dish. Sprinkle with brown sugar and 3 tablespoons butter; arrange pecans decoratively on top. Bake for 40 to 45 minutes. Let stand 5 minutes before serving.

Note: *To double the recipe, double the yam mixture ingredients; place in a deep 3-quart baking dish—keep the topping amounts (brown sugar, 3 tablespoons butter, pecans) the same. Increase baking time until yams are set in center. If using a 9" x 13" baking dish, double all the ingredients.*

Makes 6 servings. Per serving: *355 Calories; 14g Fat; 4g Protein; 54g Carbohydrate; 89mg Cholesterol; 295mg Sodium*

Green Beans Caesar

The name Caesar is a reference, not to a roman emperor, but to Caesar Cardini, a restaurant owner and chef in Tijuana, Mexico. He is credited with originating the Caesar salad in the 1920s. The flavors in this recipe—croutons and Parmesan cheese are reminiscent of that famed dish.

- 1/4 cup olive oil
- 2 teaspoons minced garlic
- 3 tablespoons lemon juice
- 2 teaspoons onion powder
- 2 teaspoons salt
- 2 10-ounce boxes frozen green beans, thawed
- 3 slices white bread, crusts trimmed, cubed
- 1/2 cup grated Parmesan cheese

Combine oil with garlic, lemon juice, onion powder, and salt.

Place green beans in ungreased 8" x 8" baking dish. Pour half of garlic-lemon oil over beans.

Toss bread cubes and cheese with remaining garlic oil; spread over beans. Bake for 20 to 25 minutes.

Makes 6 servings. Per serving: *179 Calories; 12g Fat; 6g Protein; 15g Carbohydrate; 5mg Cholesterol; 905mg Sodium*

Lemon-Herb Potato Puff

This casserole has a unique lemon flavor that you don't expect in a potato dish. Another change from the usual is having the "topping" lining the casserole instead of on top.

350°

2 pounds potatoes, peeled and quartered
3/4 cup seasoned dry bread crumbs
3 tablespoons butter, melted
1 tablespoon finely chopped fresh
or 1 teaspoon dried parsley
3 eggs, separated
1 teaspoon finely grated lemon peel
1/4 cup finely chopped fresh
or 1 tablespoon dried basil
3/4 teaspoon salt
1 cup 2% milk
1 1/2 cups shredded Swiss cheese
or other favorite cheese

Cook potatoes, covered, in boiling water 20 to 25 minutes or until tender; drain. Mash the potatoes; set aside.

In a small bowl combine bread crumbs, butter, and parsley. Press mixture onto bottom and completely up the sides of a lightly greased 1 1/2-quart casserole.

In a small bowl, beat egg yolks slightly; add lemon peel, basil, salt, and milk. Stir milk mixture into mashed potatoes. Stir in 1 cup cheese.

Beat egg whites until stiff peaks form; fold into potato mixture. Transfer to prepared casserole; top with remaining cheese. Bake for 45 minutes or until knife inserted in center comes out clean.

Note: *2 cloves garlic, minced, may be substitued for the lemon.*

Makes 8 servings. Per serving: *263 Calories; 13g Fat; 12g Protein; 25g Carbohydrate; 113mg Cholesterol; 364mg Sodium*

Patsy's Favorite Zucchini

BY PATRICIA ROSE

Another favorite casserole of Debi's mother was this zucchini dish that she would make for family get-togethers. Once she found a recipe that was wonderful, it became a "keeper."

2 cups shredded zucchini
2 1/4 cups crushed butter flavor crackers, divided
1/4 cup + 2 tablespoons butter, melted, divided
2 tablespoons onion flakes, softened in butter
1 1/2 cups low-fat shredded cheddar cheese
1 egg, beaten, or 1/4 cup Morningstar Farms® *Scramblers®*
1/4 teaspoon garlic powder
3/4 cup evaporated skim milk

Mix together zucchini, 2 cups crushed crackers, 1/4 cup butter, onion flakes, cheese, egg, garlic powder, and milk. Pat down in a greased 7" x 11" baking dish.

Mix 1/4 cup crushed crackers and 2 tablespoons butter; sprinkle on top. Bake for 35 to 45 minutes until set, bubbly, and browned.

Makes 6 servings. Per serving: *697 Calories; 41g Fat; 17g Protein; 60g Carbohydrate; 73mg Cholesterol; 1224mg Sodium*

Pecan Parmesan Noodle Casserole

Pecans are native to North America, where they were an important food source for Native American tribes in the Southeast. This side dish, which is a new spin using common ingredients, is an especially yummy combination!

350°

8 ounces medium egg noodles
1/2 cup margarine, plus extra
1 cup chopped pecans
3/4 cup chopped parsley
3 cloves garlic, minced
6 saltine crackers, crushed
Salt, to taste
1 cup grated Parmesan cheese
1 cup half-and-half
Paprika

Cook noodles according to package directions until al dente; drain and toss with a small amount of margarine.

While noodles are cooking, melt 1/2 cup margarine and sauté the pecans, parsley, garlic, and crackers for about 5 minutes.

In a greased 9" x 13" baking dish layer one-third of each of noodles and pecan mixture; salt to taste; sprinkle with one-third of the grated Parmesan cheese. Repeat the layers two more times. Pour the half-and-half over the entire casserole; then run a flat-blade knife around the edges of the dish to allow the liquid to seep down. Cover and bake for 35 minutes. Uncover and sprinkle with paprika; then bake an additional 5 minutes or until just browned on top.

Makes 6 servings. Per serving: *505 Calories; 35g Fat; 15g Protein; 34g Carbohydrate; 72mg Cholesterol; 465mg Sodium*

Refrigerator Mashed Potatoes

BY BETTY JUARROS

Until the late eighteenth century, some people thought potatoes caused leprosy.* When we made these tasty mashed potatoes, our next-door neighbor liked them so much that the recipe served only 7 of us! And he hasn't come down with leprosy yet!

- 10 medium (about 5 pounds) potatoes, peeled
- 1 8-ounce package fat-free cream cheese
- 1 cup light sour cream
- 2 teaspoons onion salt
- 1 teaspoon salt
- 2 tablespoons butter
- Paprika (optional)

Cook potatoes in boiling water until tender; drain. Mash until smooth. Add remaining ingredients and beat until light and fluffy. Cool. Place in a greased 9" x 13" baking dish. Sprinkle with paprika, if desired. Bake for 30 to 40 minutes.

Note: *This is a good recipe in which to use potatoes from the insides of Vegeburger "Boats"* *(see p. 20).*

Makes 10 servings. Per serving: *145 Calories; 3g Fat; 6g Protein; 24g Carbohydrate; 12mg Cholesterol; 677mg Sodium*

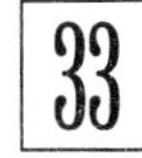

Sig. 02—M.E.O.C.

Spanakopeta (Greek Spinach Squares)

A family favorite of ours, Spanakopeta helps us keep in touch with Debi's Greek roots. Phyllo isn't as hard to work with as it may seem. Try it!

350°

3/4 cup butter, divided
1 1/2 tablespoons flour
1 cup 2% milk
1/4 teaspoon salt
2 pounds fresh spinach
1/2 small onion, finely chopped
5 eggs, beaten, or 1 1/4 cups Morningstar Farms® *Scramblers®*
1 cup finely crumbled feta cheese
Dash nutmeg (optional)
1/2 pound phyllo dough sheets, thawed

CREAM SAUCE: Melt 2 tablespoons butter in a medium saucepan, add flour, and stir until smooth. Remove from heat and gradually stir in milk. Return to heat and cook, stirring constantly, until sauce is smooth and thickened. Reduce heat and cook a few minutes longer. Stir in salt, set aside.

SPINACH FILLING: Wash spinach and discard stems. Dry as thoroughly as possible on paper towels and cut in pieces. Sauté onion in 2 tablespoons butter until soft. Add spinach and sauté a few minutes longer. Cool. Add cream sauce, eggs, cheese, and nutmeg. Mix well.

Melt remaining 1/2 cup butter. Place 6 or 7 layers of phyllo pastry sheets in a 9" x 13" baking dish, brushing each sheet well with melted butter. Add spinach mixture, then place 7 or 8 layers of phyllo pastry sheets on filling, again buttering each sheet. Bake for about 30 minutes or until crust is a golden brown. Cut into squares before serving.

Makes 12 servings. Per serving: *272 Calories; 16g Fat; 12g Protein; 21g Carbohydrate; 129mg Cholesterol; 573mg Sodium*

Spicy Baked Carrots

Did you know that we can thank the early colonists for bringing both the cultivated carrot and the lovely wildflower called Queen Anne's Lace, or "wild carrot," to the New World? But only the garden carrot was intentionally introduced. This savory carrot dish can be described as "smooth and crunchy." An unexpected combination yields a delicious outcome.

- 6 cups (about 2 pounds) 1/4" thick carrot slices
- 2 cups shredded Swiss cheese
- 1/2 cup butter, divided
- 1/2 small onion, minced
- 3 tablespoons all-purpose flour
- 1 teaspoon salt
- 1 teaspoon chili powder
- 2 cups 2% milk
- 1 cup soft bread crumbs
- 4 slices Worthington® *Stripples®*, cooked, crumbled

On stovetop or in a microwave oven, blanch carrots in a covered dish until just soft. Layer half the carrots in a greased 7" x 11" baking dish; cover with 1 cup cheese. Repeat layers.

To make the sauce, sauté onion in 1/4 cup butter for 2 minutes; blend in flour and seasonings. Cook, stirring, for 1 minute. Add milk all at once; cook, stirring until thickened. Pour sauce over carrot-cheese layers.

Melt 1/4 cup butter and combine with bread crumbs; sprinkle over all. Top with crumbled *Stripples®*. Bake for 25 minutes.

Makes 8 servings. Per serving: *406 Calories; 23g Fat; 15g Protein; 35g Carbohydrate; 61mg Cholesterol; 813mg Sodium*

Spinach-Stuffed Potatoes

Our daughter Lisa loves spinach and also twice-baked potatoes—
so we came up with this just for her!

3 large russet potatoes or 6 small potatoes, unpeeled
3 tablespoons butter
1/4 cup heavy cream
1 egg, beaten, or 1/4 cup Morningstar Farms® *Scramblers®*
1 10-ounce package frozen chopped spinach, thawed, squeezed dry
3 green onions, white part only, minced, or 1/2 teaspoon onion powder
1/2 teaspoon salt
1 cup shredded cheddar cheese

350°

Bake the potatoes in foil until just barely done (350°F for 60 to 75 minutes). Allow to cool; remove foil. Cut potatoes in half lengthwise; scoop out the insides into a large bowl, leaving a solid potato shell about 1/8" thick. Set shells in greased 9" x 13" baking dish.

Put the potato pulp through a ricer or mash with a potato masher. Beat in the butter and cream. Beat in the egg. Stir in the spinach, green onions, salt, and cheese. Spoon the mixture into the potato shells, mounding it. Bake until well browned, 30 to 35 minutes.

Makes 6 servings. Per serving: *252 Calories; 17g Fat; 10g Protein; 18g Carbohydrate; 84mg Cholesterol; 417mg Sodium*

Stuffed Zucchini

Stuffed vegetables are a popular Greek dish and always make any meal a special occasion. The filling in this version is custardlike and smooth.

- 4 medium zucchini
- 2 tablespoons olive oil
- 2 cloves garlic, minced
- 1 teaspoon onion powder
- 2 teaspoons all-purpose flour
- 1 teaspoon crushed dried basil
- 1/4 teaspoon salt
- 1/2 cup 2% milk
- 1 egg, beaten, or 1/4 cup Morningstar Farms® *Scramblers®*
- 2/3 cup grated Parmesan cheese
- 2 tablespoons butter, melted
- 1/2 cup bread crumbs

350°

Cut zucchini in half lengthwise. Place, cut side down, in a microwave-safe 9" x 1 3" baking dish. Micro-cook, covered, on 100 percent power (high) for 5 to 7 minutes or until nearly tender. (Or, cook in boiling water for 3 to 4 minutes.) Scoop out pulp, leaving a 1/4"-thick shell. Set shells back into baking dish. Finely chop the zucchini pulp and press out liquid; set aside.

In a medium saucepan, sauté garlic in hot oil until tender but not brown. Add chopped zucchini and onion powder; cook 1 minute more. Stir in flour, basil, and salt. Add milk all at once. Cook and stir until thickened and bubbly; continue for 1 minute more; let cool 10 minutes. Slowly add beaten egg to zucchini mixture, stirring constantly. Stir in Parmesan cheese. Spoon mixture into zucchini shells.

For topping, mix together the melted butter and bread crumbs; sprinkle over zucchini. Bake for 25 to 30 minutes or until filling is set. To serve, cut each zucchini in half on the diagonal and place on serving platter.

Makes 8 servings. Per serving: *153 Calories; 10g Fat; 7g Protein; 11g Carbohydrate; 41mg Cholesterol; 286mg Sodium*

Yam and Apple Casserole

What's the difference between yams and sweet potatoes? Yams have a thick skin with white, orange, or purple flesh. Sweet potatoes have a tan skin with yellow flesh OR there is a variety that looks suspiciously like a yam even though it isn't! In this recipe yams/sweet potatoes are fixed differently from your typical holiday dish, with texture and contrast added from the apples.

2 tablespoons butter
1/2 cup (packed) light brown sugar
1/2 cup dark corn syrup
1/2 teaspoon vanilla
1 teaspoon allspice
1/4 teaspoon salt
1 29-ounce can yams, drained (larger yams may be cut into smaller pieces, if desired)
3 Granny Smith apples, peeled, sliced thin

In a medium saucepan, melt butter. Add brown sugar, corn syrup, vanilla, allspice, and salt.

Stir yams and apples gently into butter mixture. Pour into a greased 8" x 8" baking dish. Bake about 60 minutes.

Makes 6 servings. Per serving: *295 Calories; 4g Fat; 0g Protein; 67g Carbohydrate; 10mg Cholesterol; 199mg Sodium*

Yellow Squash Delight

Every year squash seems to do well in our garden. However, one year we had a bumper crop of yellow squash. We were trying every squash recipe we could find. This one came out a winner.

- 2 pounds yellow squash, sliced
- 1 medium onion, finely chopped
- 1 can condensed low-fat cream of celery soup
- 1 pint light sour cream
- 2 ounces pimiento, chopped
- 1 can sliced water chestnuts, drained, chopped
- 3 3/4 cups or 1 6-ounce package herb-seasoned stuffing
- 1/2 cup butter, melted
- 1 cup shredded low-fat cheddar cheese

Cook squash and onion in water until tender; drain. Put into mixing bowl; add soup, sour cream, pimiento, and water chestnuts. Mix and set aside.

Mix the stuffing with the melted butter. Use half of the stuffing to line a greased 9" x 13" baking dish. Pour the squash mixture over the layer of stuffing; then use the rest of the stuffing for topping. Sprinkle with cheese. Bake for 45 minutes.

Makes 12 servings. Per serving: *277 Calories; 10g Fat; 9g Protein; 34g Carbohydrate; 27mg Cholesterol; 1275mg Sodium*

Chapter 2: 375 Degrees

Entrees

Side Dishes

Baked Lentils With Cheese

Lentils are one of the oldest foods known. They were the main ingredient in Esau and Jacob's "pottage" (see Genesis 25:34). This recipe came from a Mennonite cookbook given us by Debi's Aunt Martha.

- 1 3/4 cups lentils, rinsed
- 2 cups water
- 1 whole bay leaf
- 2 teaspoons salt
- 1/8 teaspoon dried marjoram
- 1/8 teaspoon dried sage
- 1/8 teaspoon dried thyme
- 2 cloves garlic, minced
- 1 medium onion, finely chopped, or 1 tablespoon dehydrated onion
- 2 cups canned or 1 14.5-ounce can tomatoes
- 2 large carrots, sliced 1/8" thick
- 1/2 cup thinly sliced celery
- 2 tablespoons finely chopped parsley
- 3 cups shredded cheddar cheese

Combine lentils, water, seasonings, garlic, onion, and tomatoes in 9" x 13" baking dish. Cover tightly and bake 30 minutes. Uncover and stir in carrots and celery. Bake, covered, 40 minutes until vegetables are tender. Stir in parsley. Sprinkle cheese on top. Bake, uncovered, 5 minutes until cheese melts.

Makes 8 servings. Per serving: *342 Calories; 15g Fat; 24g Protein; 31g Carbohydrate; 45mg Cholesterol; 987mg Sodium*

Chicken Florentine

Debi likes to find special yet easy entrees to make for the holidays. Using puff pastry always gives an elegant appearance. In case you've wondered, as early as the sixteenth century, chefs from Florence were known for using spinach in their recipes—hence the word *Florentine,* indicating the presence of spinach.

375°

- 1 16-ounce package frozen puff pastry sheets
- 3 tablespoons butter
- 2 12.5-ounce cans Worthington® *Low Fat FriChik®*, split lengthwise
- 2 9-ounce packages frozen creamed spinach, thawed
- 1/2 cup (plus extra for garnish) grated Parmesan cheese
- 1/2 cup pine nuts, toasted, chopped
- 1 tablespoon chopped fresh or 1/2 teaspoon dried basil
- 2 cloves garlic, minced
- 1 egg or 1/4 cup Morningstar Farms® *Scramblers®*
- 1 tablespoon water

Thaw pastry 20 minutes.

In large skillet, brown *FriChik®* in butter; set aside.

In medium bowl, combine spinach, Parmesan cheese, pine nuts, basil, and garlic.

Roll one pastry sheet on a lightly floured surface to a 12" square; cut into four 6" squares. Spoon one-eighth of the spinach mixture in center of each square. Top with 2 1/2 pieces of *FriChik®*, laying lengthwise over spinach. Moisten top edge of pastry square with water and bring bottom and top to meet in center over chicken, pressing gently to seal. Moisten side edges and fold up to seal. Repeat steps with remaining ingredients. Place seam side down on ungreased baking sheet.

Make egg wash by beating egg with water. Brush pastry with egg wash and sprinkle with additional Parmesan cheese. Bake for 25 minutes or until golden.

Makes 8 servings. Per serving: *413 Calories; 17g Fat; 19g Protein; 43g Carbohydrate; 50 mg Cholesterol; 939mg Sodium*

Chicken With Potato "Stuffing"

A cross between mashed potatoes and bread stuffing, this casserole makes a nice change-of-pace holiday addition.

1/2 cup butter, divided
1/2 medium onion, finely chopped
1 cup finely chopped celery
4 cups mashed potatoes
2 eggs, lightly beaten, or 1/2 cup Morningstar Farms® *Scramblers®*
1 cup soft bread cubes
1/2 teaspoon poultry seasoning
1/4 cup chopped fresh parsley
1 teaspoon salt
2 12-ounce cans Worthington® *Low Fat FriChik®*, halved lengthwise
1/2 teaspoon paprika

Melt 6 tablespoons butter in large skillet; sauté onion and celery for 5 minutes. Turn into mixing bowl. Add remaining ingredients, except for *FriChik®* and paprika; mix well. Spread in a greased 8" x 11" baking dish. Arrange chicken pieces on stuffing. Dot with remaining butter. Sprinkle with paprika. Cover and bake for 30 minutes; uncover and bake for 10 minutes more.

Makes 8 servings. Per serving: *378 Calories; 18g Fat; 14g Protein; 41g Carbohydrate; 86mg Cholesterol; 1167mg Sodium*

Macaroni Romanoff

More than 500 different pasta shapes have been identified!* Of course, you won't find quite that large of a selection at your local supermarket. But be creative and try something new in this creamy and savory recipe.

375°

- 4 cups (or 1 pound) elbow macaroni
- 3 tablespoons butter
- 1/2 medium onion, thinly sliced, or 2 teaspoons onion powder
- 2 cloves garlic, crushed
- 3 cups light sour cream
- 2 cups low-fat cottage cheese
- 1 cup 2% milk
- 1/4 cup chopped fresh or 4 teaspoons dried parsley
- 1 tablespoon poppy seeds
- 1 1/2 teaspoons salt

Cook macaroni in salted water in a 4 1/2-quart pan for only 5 to 6 minutes. Drain.

In same pan, melt butter over low heat. Add onion and garlic (if using onion powder, add with next step); sauté until tender. Mix in remaining ingredients except macaroni. Add macaroni and mix well. Pour into a greased 9" x 13" baking dish. Cover and bake for 25 to 30 minutes or until hot and bubbly. Remove cover; bake 5 minutes more. Serve immediately.

Makes 12 servings. Per serving: *225 Calories; 6g Fat; 12g Protein; 30g Carbohydrate; 17mg Cholesterol; 499mg Sodium*

Mexican Casserole With Spinach

Did you know that spinach was the first frozen vegetable to be sold?*
As an ingredient, here it adds a unique twist to this south-of-the-border dish.

- 1 20-ounce can Worthington® Low Fat Vegetarian Burger
- 1 medium onion, chopped, or 1 tablespoon dehydrated onion flakes
- 1 package taco seasoning mix
- 1 cup water
- 1/2 teaspoon garlic powder
- 1 cup medium hot taco sauce
- 10 corn tortillas
- 2 10-ounce packages frozen chopped spinach, thawed and squeezed dry
- 3 cups shredded low-fat Monterey Jack cheese
- 1 cup light sour cream

375°

Cook burger, onion, taco seasoning, water, and garlic powder until onions are tender.

Put 1/2 cup taco sauce in bottom of a greased 9" x 13" baking dish. Coat tortillas in it. Tear 5 of the tortillas into smaller pieces and spread on bottom of baking dish.

Put half the spinach in burger mixture. Spread mixture over tortillas. Top with half of the cheese and sour cream. Continue layering with rest of tortillas, sauce, spinach, sour cream, and cheese. Cover and bake for 25 minutes. Uncover, bake 20 minutes longer.

Makes 12 servings. Per serving: *219 Calories; 10g Fat; 17g Protein; 16g Carbohydrate; 202mg Cholesterol; 646mg Sodium*

Old-Fashioned Steak Roast

FROM JEANNE PEDERSEN

Jim grew up having this old-fashioned roast as part of a special family meal. We actually have his great-grandmother's oval baking dish with etched metal casserole holder in which it was often served!

375°

- 2 medium potatoes, grated
- 1 cup 2% milk
- 1/3 cup chopped onions or 1 tablespoon dried onions, rehydrated
- 1 20-ounce can Worthington® Vegetable Steaks, chopped or grated
- 1/4 cup oil
- 2 eggs, slightly beaten, or 1/2 cup Morningstar Farms® *Scramblers®*
- 1/2 teaspoon celery salt
- 1/2 teaspoon poultry seasoning
- 1 teaspoon garlic powder

Combine potatoes and milk, allowing the potatoes to soak for 5 minutes. Add remaining ingredients and mix well. Place in a greased 8" x 8" baking dish. Bake for 60 minutes.

Makes 6 servings. Per serving: *227 Calories; 13g Fat; 17g Protein; 13g Carbohydrate; 74mg Cholesterol; 426mg Sodium*

Pastitsio

Pastitsio is a Greek macaroni pie that uses quite a few pots and pans to make, but it's well worth it! By the way, the accent falls on the second syllable.

- 2 tablespoons olive oil
- 1/2 medium onion, finely chopped, or 2 teaspoons dried onion, rehydrated
- 1 clove garlic, minced
- 1 20-ounce can Worthington® Low Fat Vegetarian Burger
- 1/8 teaspoon cinnamon
- 1 8-ounce can tomato sauce
- 5 tablespoons butter, divided
- 1/4 cup flour
- 2 cups 2% milk
- 1/2 teaspoon salt
- Pinch nutmeg
- 1/3 cup grated Parmesan cheese
- 8 ounces small elbow macaroni
- 2 eggs or 1/2 cup Morningstar Farms® *Scramblers®*
- 2 cups shredded kasseri or kefalotiri cheese

Sauté onion and garlic in the olive oil until soft. Crumble in the burger. Cook, stirring, until burger browns slightly. Stir in cinnamon and tomato sauce; set aside.

Melt 3 tablespoons butter in saucepan and stir in flour. Add milk gradually and cook, stirring constantly, until thickened. Add salt, nutmeg, and Parmesan cheese.

Meanwhile, cook macaroni in boiling salted water 10 to 12 minutes, or until tender. Drain well; let cool 5 minutes; put back in pot. Add eggs and 2 tablespoons butter. Beat briskly with spoon until well mixed.

In a greased 9" x 13" baking dish, layer ingredients as follows: half the macaroni, all the burger mixture, half the cheese, remaining macaroni, then the white sauce (whisk sauce again before pouring). Shake dish gently to settle white sauce. Sprinkle on remaining cheese, dot with butter (if desired), and sprinkle with additional nutmeg. Bake for 45 to 55 minutes or until browned and set.

Note: *If the Greek cheeses are unavailable, grated Parmesan or Romano may be substituted.*

Makes 12 servings. Per serving: *321 Calories; 17g Fat; 18g Protein; 23g Carbohydrate; 70mg Cholesterol; 850mg Sodium*

Pecan Chicken Loaf

Did you know that the state nut of Alabama is the pecan; the state tree of Texas is the pecan tree; and the largest producer of pecans in the U.S. is the state of Georgia?* This tasty and nutritious loaf, which contains pecans, received rave reviews at our office.

375°

- 1/4 cup butter
- 1 small onion, finely chopped, or 2 teaspoons onion powder
- 6 eggs or 1 1/2 cups Morningstar Farms® *Scramblers®*
- 1/2 cup 2% milk
- 1 cup chopped pecans
- 1 13-ounce can Worthington® Meatless Chicken Diced, drained
- 1/2 cup raw rolled oats
- 1 packet G. Washington's® Golden Seasoning and Broth
- 2 cups low-fat cottage cheese
- 3 tablespoons chickenlike seasoning and broth mix
- 1/2 cup wheat germ
- 3 cups Kellogg's® *Special K®* cereal

Sauté onion in butter until soft. Remove from heat.

In large mixing bowl, lightly beat eggs with milk. Add remaining ingredients, including onions. Carefully mix until blended. Cover and bake in a greased 9" x 13" baking dish for 60 minutes. Remove cover and bake an additional 15 minutes.

Makes 12 servings. Per serving: *252 Calories; 14g Fat; 16g Protein; 16g Carbohydrate; 120mg Cholesterol; 889mg Sodium*

Roasted Linguini Casserole

Will Rogers once said, "An onion can make people cry, but there has never been a vegetable invented to make them laugh."* The hearty flavor of these roasted vegetables will bring at least a smile to your face. Another reason to smile is that the recipe feeds a large group!

- 2 zucchini
- 2 yellow squash
- 8 ounces fresh mushrooms, quartered
- 3 tablespoons balsamic vinegar
- 1 tablespoon olive oil
- 2 cloves garlic, minced
- 1/2 teaspoon crushed dried rosemary
- 1 16-ounce package linguini
- 1 14.5-ounce can Worthington® *Low Fat FriChik®*, chopped
- 2 bunches fresh spinach, washed and chopped, or 1 10-ounce package frozen chopped spinach, thawed and drained
- 1 16-ounce jar alfredo sauce
- 1 15-ounce container low-fat ricotta cheese
- Dash hot pepper sauce
- 1 cup shredded part-skim-milk mozzarella cheese
- 1/4 cup grated Parmesan cheese

Cut squashes in half lengthwise then crosswise into 1/2" pieces. Place squash and mushrooms in a greased 9" x 13" baking dish.

In a small dish, combine vinegar, oil, garlic, and rosemary; brush evenly over vegetables. Bake for 15 minutes; stir. Continue baking until vegetables are browned and tender, about 15 more minutes.

While vegetables are baking, prepare linguini according to package directions.

In large bowl, combine all remaining ingredients except mozzarella and Parmesan cheeses. Add roasted vegetables and 3/4 cup of the vegetable juices. Spread mixture in a greased 10" x 15" baking dish. Sprinkle cheeses over casserole. Cover with foil; bake 45 minutes. Remove cover and bake 5 to 10 more minutes till cheese is browned.

Makes 16 servings. Per serving: *253 Calories; 9g Fat; 13g Protein; 29g Carbohydrate; 33mg Cholesterol; 388mg Sodium*

Russian-Style Meat Pies

These pies remind us of the kinds of food served to us on an evangelistic trip to Russia. The use of cabbage, both red and green, as well as sour cream, was a common occurance.

375°

2 tablespoons oil
1/2 pound Morningstar Farms™ *Ground Meatless®* Crumbles, thawed
1/2 cup chopped onion or 2 tablespoons dried onion flakes, rehydrated
6 cloves garlic, minced
2 tablespoons dried parsley
1 16-ounce can sweet-sour red cabbage, drained
3/4 teaspoon salt
1 16-ounce loaf frozen white bread dough (thawed according to package directions)
Sour cream, for dipping

In skillet cook burger, onion, and garlic in oil until meat is browned. Stir in parsley, cabbage, and salt. Set aside.

Divide thawed bread dough evenly into 16 portions. On lightly floured surface, roll each piece into a 4" circle. Place a scant 1/4 cup of the burger mixture onto half of each circle of dough. Moisten edges of the dough with water; fold over. Seal edges by pressing with fingers or a fork. Place on a greased baking sheet. Let rise, covered, in warm place about 30 minutes. Bake for 15 to 20 minutes. Serve with sour cream.

Makes 16 servings. Per serving: *124 Calories; 3g Fat; 5g Protein; 19g Carbohydrate; 0mg Cholesterol; 425mg Sodium*

Savory Veggie Dogs and Noodles

Kids especially seem to enjoy the combination of noodles and hot dogs. Some of those who taste-tested this recipe thought the "Dogs" tasted like the "real thing"!

2 cups medium-size noodles
1/4 cup butter, divided
1 cup finely chopped onions, or 2 tablespoons onion powder
1 16-ounce package Morningstar Farms™ *Veggie Dog®* links, thinly sliced
6 eggs, slightly beaten, or 1 1/2 cups Morningstar Farms® *Scramblers®*
2 cups light sour cream
1 cup low-fat cottage cheese
1/2 teaspoon salt
1 cup Kellogg's® Corn Flake Crumbs

Cook noodles according to directions on the package; drain.

Cook onion and *Veggie Dog®* slices in 2 tablespoons butter until onions are tender and slices are lightly browned. Combine *Veggie Dog®* slices, noodles, eggs, sour cream, cottage cheese, and salt; pour into greased 2-quart baking dish.

Melt 2 tablespoons butter and combine with Corn Flake Crumbs; sprinkle over top. Bake for 40 to 45 minutes. Let stand 10 minutes; cut into squares.

Makes 8 servings. Per serving: *288 Calories; 12g Fat; 23g Protein; 20g Carbohydrate; 191mg Cholesterol; 980mg Sodium*

Shepherd's Pie

Shepherd's Pie, a mashed-potato-topped meat dish, was originally created as an economical way to use leftovers from the Sunday roast. You don't need to be a shepherd to enjoy this simple dish.

375°

- 3 large or 6 small potatoes
- 6 cloves garlic, peeled
- 2 tablespoons oil
- 1 16-ounce package Morningstar Farms™ *Ground Meatless*® Crumbles, thawed
- 1 medium onion, finely chopped, or 1 tablespoon dried onion, rehydrated
- 1 teaspoon garlic powder
- 1 teaspoon oregano
- 1/2 teaspoon Vegex® yeast paste
- 1 cup hot water
- 2 eggs, slightly beaten, or 1/2 cup Morningstar Farms® *Scramblers*®
- 2 tablespoons butter
- 1/2 teaspoon salt
- 1/4 cup low-fat evaporated milk
- 1 cup shredded low-fat cheddar cheese
- Paprika

Peel potatoes; halve and place in a medium saucepan. Add garlic cloves and cover with water. Cook until potatoes are tender.

Meanwhile, sauté burger and onion in oil until onion is transparent. Add garlic powder and oregano.

Dissolve Vegex® in hot water and add to burger. Let cool. Stir in eggs.

To make mashed potatoes, drain water from potatoes. Mash potatoes, garlic, butter, salt, and evaporated milk until smooth.

To assemble, place burger mixture in a greased 7" x 11" baking dish. Smooth mashed potatoes over top. Sprinkle with cheese and paprika. Bake for 30 minutes.

Makes 6 servings. Per serving: *294 Calories; 12g Fat; 22g Protein; 20g Carbohydrate; 87mg Cholesterol; 827mg Sodium*

Skallops in Baked Cream

This entree is "oh my goodness" yummy! It is rich. We just had to put it in, it's so good. We tend to agree with the person who said, "There is no such thing as a little garlic!"*

3/4 cup butter flavor cracker crumbs
1 1/2 teaspoons salt
1/2 teaspoon crushed dried basil
1/2 teaspoon dried oregano
1 tablespoon finely chopped fresh
  or 1 teaspoon dried parsley

2 20-ounce cans Worthington®
  Vegetable Skallops®
  or Loma Linda® *Tender Bits*
2 cups heavy cream
2 cloves garlic, crushed

In a large zippered plastic bag, combine crumbs, salt, basil, oregano, and parsley. Shake *Skallops®* in the crumb mixture to coat. Spread in greased 7" x 11" baking dish.

In small bowl, mix cream and garlic; pour over *Skallops®*. Bake for 40 to 45 minutes or until bubbling and lightly browned.

Makes 8 servings. Per serving: *339 Calories; 24g Fat; 17g Protein; 14g Carbohydrate; 82mg Cholesterol; 836mg Sodium*

Steaks Deluxe

Before the days of automation, gluten steaks were cut and trimmed by hand. Debi's grandfather, Arthur Rose, worked for Loma Linda Foods. He created the machinery that would slice the products uniformly.

375°

- 1 50-ounce can Worthington® *Multi-Grain Cutlets®*, drained (reserve liquid)
- 2 eggs, beaten, or 1/2 cup Morningstar Farms® *Scramblers®*
- 3/4 cup cracker meal or breading meal
- 1/4 cup oil, divided
- 2 tablespoons butter
- 1 pound fresh mushrooms, sliced
- 3 cups light sour cream
- 1/2 teaspoon garlic powder
- 1 teaspoon onion powder
- 1 packet G. Washington's® Rich Brown Seasoning and Broth
- 2 teaspoons Vegex® yeast paste
- 2 cups shredded low-fat Monterey Jack cheese

Dip *Cutlets®* in eggs then breading meal.

In large skillet, brown half the cutlets in 2 tablespoons of the oil; repeat. Lay the browned *Cutlets®* in a greased 9" x 13" baking dish, making 2 rows and overlapping as needed.

Use the same skillet for making the sauce. Sauté mushrooms in butter.

Combine sour cream and 1 1/3 cup liquid from dinner cuts; add to mushrooms. Blend in seasonings and Vegex®. Bring to a boil. Pour sauce over the *Cutlets®* and cover with cheese. Cover and bake for 45 minutes.

Note: *The sauce in this dish makes it perfect to serve with hot, buttered noodles.*

Makes 14 servings. Per serving: *233 Calories; 12g Fat; 18g Protein; 12g Carbohydrate; 153mg Cholesterol; 595mg Sodium*

Tofu Croquettes

Legend has it that tofu was developed by prince Liu An (179-122 B.C.) while searching for a substance to help him achieve immortality.* In this recipe, the contrast of crunchy on the outside and soft on the inside makes these balls a delicious way to fix the humble tofu.

4 eggs or 1 cup Morningstar Farms® *Scramblers®*, divided
1 tablespoon oil
2 12-ounce packages low-fat firm tofu, crumbled fine
1/2 medium onion, finely chopped, or 1 1/2 teaspoon dried onion, rehydrated
2 teaspoons Vegex® yeast paste
1 teaspoon Bakon Seasoning®
1/4 cup raw rolled oats
1 teaspoon salt
2 tablespoons brewer's yeast
4 cloves garlic, minced
2 cups (as needed) Kellogg's® Corn Flake Crumbs

In a small bowl, beat 2 eggs.

Scramble the beaten eggs in a small frying pan in oil until light brown; place in mixing bowl. To the scrambled eggs add all the remaining ingredients except the Corn Flake Crumbs; mix well. Refrigerate overnight. Shape into walnut-sized balls; then roll in corn flake crumbs. Place on greased baking sheet. Bake for 20 minutes or until golden brown.

Makes 8 servings. Per serving: *130 Calories; 5g Fat; 11g Protein; 10g Carbohydrate; 106mg Cholesterol; 526mg Sodium*

Vegeburger Roast

Using two kinds of nuts adds a great flavor, as well as extra protein, to the basic "meatloaf." If there are any leftovers of this tasty roast, you'll have the makings of a good sandwich filling!

375°

1/4 cup margarine
1 cup finely chopped onion
  or 1/4 cup dried onion, rehydrated
1 cup finely chopped celery (about 2 stalks)
2 cloves garlic, minced
5 eggs, slightly beaten, or 1 1/4 cups
  Morningstar Farms® *Scramblers®*
2 20-ounce cans Worthington® Low Fat
  Vegetarian Burger
1 cup finely chopped pecans
3/4 cup finely chopped salted cashews
1/2 cup dry bread crumbs
1/2 teaspoon thyme
1/4 teaspoon nutmeg

Melt margarine in a skillet. Add onion, celery, and garlic. Cover and cook at medium heat until vegetables are tender but not brown. Combine cooked vegetable mixture with remaining ingredients. Mix until well blended. Pour into a greased 9" x 13" baking dish. Cover and bake for 60 minutes, removing the cover during the last 10 minutes. Serve with favorite sauce or gravy.

Makes 12 servings. Per serving: *277 Calories; 19g Fat; 20g Protein; 10g Carbohydrate; 89mg Cholesterol; 532mg Sodium*

Apple Pecan Stuffing

An old proverb says, "An apple a day keeps the doctor away!" Perhaps that's why the average American eats almost 20 pounds of fresh apples each year.* In this stuffing, apples add a fresh, sweet taste to an old favorite.

6 tablespoons butter, divided
2/3 cup diced onion
2/3 cup diced celery
4 slices day-old bread, cubed
3 cups diced apples
1 teaspoon salt
1/2 teaspoon poultry seasoning
1 tablespoon chopped fresh or 1 teaspoon dried parsley
1/2 cup chopped pecans
2 eggs, slightly beaten, or 1/2 cup Morningstar Farms® *Scramblers*®

Melt 1/4 cup butter in skillet. Add onion and celery and sauté for 5 minutes.

Place bread cubes in large mixing bowl; add sautéed vegetables.

Melt 2 tablespoons butter in same skillet. Stir in apples and cook until golden, about 5 minutes. Add apples to bread mixture. Mix in salt, poultry seasoning, parsley, and pecans. Add eggs and mix thoroughly. Spread stuffing in a greased 7" x 11" baking dish. Cover and bake for 30 minutes; uncover and bake for 10 minutes more.

Makes 6 servings. Per serving: *272 Calories; 20g Fat; 5g Protein; 21g Carbohydrate; 102mg Cholesterol; 594mg Sodium*

Apricot Sweet Potatoes

Apricots were once thought to have originated in Armenia. It has been recently discovered that they actually came from China. Apricots, both pieces and nectar, add a new twist to a traditional holiday dish. Being easy to prepare is a bonus!

375°

- 1 1/4 cups brown sugar
- 1 1/2 tablespoons cornstarch
- 1/4 teaspoon salt
- 1/8 teaspoon cinnamon
- 1 teaspoon shredded orange peel
- 1 16-ounce can apricot halves in light syrup, drained
- 1 cup apricot nectar
- 2 tablespoons butter
- 1/2 cup seedless raisins
- 1/2 cup chopped pecans
- 2 29-ounce cans sweet potatoes, halved lengthwise

In a medium saucepan, combine brown sugar, cornstarch, salt, cinnamon, orange peel, apricots, apricot nectar, butter, and raisins. Bring to a boil. Simmer until slightly thickened.

Place sweet potatoes in a greased 7" x 11" baking dish. Pour fruit mixture over potatoes and top with pecans. Bake for 25 to 30 minutes.

Makes 10 servings. Per serving: *390 Calories; 6g Fat; 1g Protein; 86g Carbohydrate; 6mg Cholesterol; 127mg Sodium*

Artichoke Florentine

Artichokes were once called "one of the earth's monstrosities."* In the sixteenth century, Catherine de Medici is said to have introduced them to Italy, where her Florentine chefs also liked using spinach in their cuisine. This dish would have made them all happy!

- 1/4 cup butter, divided
- 1/2 pound fresh mushrooms, chopped
- 1 tablespoon flour
- 1/2 cup 2% milk
- 2 10-ounce packages frozen chopped spinach, cooked and drained
- 1/2 teaspoon salt
- 1/4 teaspoon garlic powder
- 2 13.75-ounce cans artichoke hearts (trimmed of any remnants of outer leaves)
- 1/2 cup light sour cream
- 1/2 cup light mayonnaise
- 1/4 cup lemon juice

Sauté mushrooms in 2 tablespoons butter.

Melt remaining 2 tablespoons butter in 2-quart saucepan. Add flour and stir until smooth. Remove from heat and gradually add milk. Return to heat and cook until thickened, stirring constantly. Add mushrooms, spinach, and seasonings.

Place artichoke hearts in greased 7" x 11" baking dish; cover with spinach mixture.

Prepare sauce with sour cream, mayonnaise, and lemon juice. Pour over artichoke mixture. Bake for 30 minutes.

Makes 12 servings. Per serving: *79 Calories; 5g Fat; 3g Protein; 7g Carbohydrate; 16mg Cholesterol; 424mg Sodium*

Broccoli Phyllo Bundles

Broccoli was developed some 2,500 years ago on the island of Cypress.* Phyllo dough also comes from the Mediterranean area. Together they make a special treat flavored here with other ingredients used in that region.

- 1 tablespoon olive oil
- 1 clove garlic, minced
- 4 cups (about 2 medium crowns) small broccoli florets
- 1/2 medium onion, finely chopped, or 1 1/2 teaspoons onion powder
- 2 tablespoons snipped parsley
- 1/2 package (10 sheets) phyllo dough, thawed
- 6 tablespoons butter, melted
- 1 cup crumbled feta cheese

Preheat a large fry pan over high heat. Add oil. Stir-fry garlic for 30 seconds. Add broccoli; stir-fry for 4 minutes. Add onion; stir-fry for 2 minutes more. Stir in parsley.

Stack 5 phyllo sheets, buttering each sheet. Cut stacked phyllo into quarters. Repeat with other 5 phyllo sheets. Place equal amounts of the broccoli mixture and feta in the center of each phyllo section. Form each into a bundle by bringing phyllo points up to the top of mixture, pressing points together, and twisting slightly. Place on an ungreased baking sheet; brush the outside with remaining butter. Bake for 20 to 25 minutes or until golden.

Makes 8 servings. Per serving: *245 Calories; 14g Fat; 7g Protein; 23g Carbohydrate; 36mg Cholesterol; 447mg Sodium*

Cheesy Potato Crisps

The terms *Big Wheel* and *Big Cheese* originally referred to those who were wealthy enough to purchase a whole wheel of cheese.[A] In today's world, a wheel of cheese would take up a lot of space in our refrigerators! The smaller blocks of cheese work just fine!

- 1/4 cup butter
- 4 large potatoes, scrubbed
- 1 1/2 cups Kellogg's® Corn Flake Crumbs
- 3/4 cup shredded sharp cheddar cheese
- 1 1/2 teaspoons salt
- 3/4 teaspoon paprika

375°

Melt butter in a jelly-roll pan in the oven.

Cut potatoes in slices lengthwise, about 1/4" thick. Arrange in single layer in pan, turning once to coat both sides with butter.

Combine Corn Flake Crumbs, cheese, salt, and paprika. Sprinkle over potatoes. Bake for 30 minutes until done and topping is lightly browned and cripsy.

Makes 6 servings. Per serving: *208 Calories; 12g Fat; 6g Protein; 19g Carbohydrate; 35mg Cholesterol; 762mg Sodium*

Chile Cheese Rice Casserole

Did you know that 50 percent of all the world's rice is eaten within 8 miles of where it is grown?* However, you don't need to live near any rice fields to enjoy this savory casserole.

375°

2 tablespoons butter
1 cup finely chopped onion
  or 1 tablespoon onion powder
4 cups cooked rice
2 cups light sour cream
1 cup low-fat cottage cheese
1/2 teaspoon salt
1 7-ounce can diced green chiles
2 cups grated sharp cheddar cheese

In small skillet, sauté onion in butter until golden, about 5 minutes. (If using onion powder, add at the next step.)

In a large bowl, mix all ingredients thoroughly. Spread in a greased 9" x 13" baking dish. Bake for 35 to 45 minutes or until hot and bubbly.

Makes 12 servings. Per serving: *216 Calories; 10g Fat; 10g Protein; 23g Carbohydrate; 30mg Cholesterol; 355mg Sodium*

Corn Pudding

Corn, or maize, most likely was domesticated in central Mexico. The oldest remains of corn found at archaeological sites there resemble popcorn-type corn.* Using the modern convenience of canned corn here makes this dish easy to assemble.

1/2 cup butter, melted
1 14.5-ounce can creamed corn
1 15.5-ounce can whole kernel corn, drained
1 cup light sour cream
2 eggs, beaten, or 1/2 cup Morningstar Farms® *Scramblers®*
1 7.5-ounce package corn muffin mix

Mix all ingredients. Pour into a greased 8" x 8" baking dish. Bake for 60 minutes.

Makes 6 servings. Per serving: *421 Calories; 22g Fat; 7g Protein; 48g Carbohydrate; 115mg Cholesterol; 968mg Sodium*

Greek Zucchini Gratin

The Mediterranean area is the source of many rich culinary flavors. This dish uses a number of ingredients often used in Greek cooking: zucchini, fresh mint, feta cheese, and Kalamata olives.

375°

- 2 pounds zucchini (about 4 medium), scrubbed, trimmed, and coarsely grated
- 3 eggs, beaten lightly, or 3/4 cup Morningstar Farms® *Scramblers®*
- 5 scallions, sliced thin
- 1/2 cup finely chopped fresh parsley
- 1/2 cup finely chopped fresh mint leaves
- 1 1/2 cups shredded fontina cheese (about 8 ounces), divided
- 1/4 cup crumbled feta cheese (about 2 ounces)
- 1 teaspoon salt
- 1 1/4 cups flour
- 1 cup fresh coarse bread crumbs
- 1/4 cup butter, cut into bits
- 20 Kalamata olives, pitted, halved

In a large bowl, stir together the zucchini, eggs, scallions, parsley, mint, 1 cup of the fontina, feta, and salt. Add the flour gradually, stirring. Spread the mixture evenly in a greased 9" x 13" baking dish. Sprinkle with the bread crumbs and the remaining 1/2 cup fontina, dot with the butter, and arrange the olives decoratively on top. Bake for 35 to 40 minutes or until the top is golden.

Note: *Gruyère cheese can be substituted for the fontina cheese.*

Makes 12 servings. Per serving: *194 Calories; 12g Fat; 8g Protein; 15g Carbohydrate; 82mg Cholesterol; 512mg Sodium*

Green Beans and Friends

Jim Davis, the creator of "Garfield," once said: "Vegetables are a 'must' on a diet. I suggest carrot cake, zucchini bread, and pumpkin pie."* We'd like to suggest this great medley of vegetables, without any sugar!

- 1 16-ounce package frozen French-cut green beans
- 1 8-ounce package frozen artichoke hearts
- 1 8-ounce can sliced water chestnuts, drained
- 2 ounces pimiento strips
- 1/4 cup butter
- 1/2 cup chopped white onion
- 1 cup sliced fresh mushrooms or 1 6-ounce can sliced mushrooms, drained
- 2 cloves garlic, crushed
- 1/4 cup flour
- 1 teaspoon salt
- 2 cups 2% milk
- 1 teaspoon soy sauce
- 1 cup shredded low-fat Monterey Jack cheese
- 1 2.8-ounce can French fried onions
- 1/2 cup shredded low-fat cheddar cheese, optional

Thaw green beans and artichoke hearts; drain. Cut artichoke hearts in half.

In a greased 2-quart baking dish, layer half of each: green beans, artichoke hearts, water chestnuts, and pimientos. Repeat layers.

In a 2-quart saucepan melt butter. Sauté onion and mushrooms 3 minutes; add garlic and sauté 2 minutes longer or until onion is tender. Stir in flour and salt. Remove from heat, gradually add milk. Cook over medium heat, stirring constantly, until thickened. Cook 2 minutes longer; remove from heat. Add soy sauce and Monterey Jack cheese and stir until cheese is melted. Pour sauce over vegetables. Bake for 30 minutes. Top with French fried onions and cheddar cheese (if desired). Bake 5 minutes longer.

Makes 8 servings. Per serving: *261 Calories; 15g Fat; 9g Protein; 18g Carbohydrate; 121mg Cholesterol; 629mg Sodium*

Sig. 03—M.E.O.C.

Oniony Spinach Rice

American poet Carl Sandburg said, "Life is like an onion: You peel off one layer at a time and sometimes you weep."* For those of you who like onions, this is a recipe you must try. Fortunately, using dry onion soup mix means there aren't any tears!

- 3 cups cooked rice (cooked in vegetable broth, if desired)
- 2 eggs, beaten, or 1/2 cup Morningstar Farms® *Scramblers®*
- 1 cup shredded low-fat cheddar cheese
- 1 10-ounce package frozen chopped spinach, thawed and drained
- 1 envelope onion soup mix
- 2 cups light sour cream
- 2 tablespoons chopped pimientos

Mix all ingredients well. Place in a greased 7" x 11" baking dish. Bake for 25 to 30 minutes or until bubbly.

Makes 8 servings. Per serving: *199 Calories; 4g Fat; 10g Protein; 27g Carbohydrate; 61mg Cholesterol; 581mg Sodium*

Potato Alfredo

Contrary to popular belief, Washington State is actually the number one producer of potatoes in the U.S. Idaho is second, followed by Wisconsin, which is the largest producer of red potatoes. Wanting a new twist to this common vegetable, Debi came up with this easy recipe. Using a food processor for the potatoes and cheese makes this a quick fix. Parboiling the potatoes turns it into a great make-ahead dish.

10 medium potatoes
1 teaspoon salt
1 16-ounce jar roasted garlic alfredo pasta sauce
2 cups low-fat ricotta cheese
3 cups (1 12-ounce package) shredded part-skim-milk mozzarella cheese
1/2 cup grated Parmesan cheese

375°

Peel and slice potatoes 1/4 inch thick. In a medium saucepan of boiling water, boil potatoes for 5 minutes, until just tender; drain.

In a greased 9" x 13" baking dish, layer half of each: potatoes, salt, sauce, ricotta, and mozzarella. Repeat layers with remaining ingredients. Sprinkle Parmesan cheese on top. Cover and bake for 60 minutes, removing cover the last 15 minutes.

Makes 12 servings. Per serving: *272 Calories; 14g Fat; 16g Protein; 22g Carbohydrate; 57mg Cholesterol; 693mg Sodium*

Potato-Crust Quiche

What a great way to use up leftover mashed potatoes! Think of your favorite vegetable-and-cheese combination, and use it in this unique side dish.

- 3 medium potatoes, scrubbed and halved
- 1/4 cup butter, softened
- 3 3/4 cups (16-ounce bag) frozen chopped broccoli (or vegetable of choice), thawed, well drained
- 1 cup shredded low-fat cheddar cheese
- 1 cup evaporated low-fat milk
- 3 eggs, beaten, or 3/4 cup Morningstar Farms® *Scramblers®*
- 1 tablespoon flour
- 1/2 teaspoon salt
- 1/2 teaspoon onion powder
- 1/2 teaspoon dried savory or dried basil

Cook potatoes, covered, in boiling salted water until tender. Drain; peel; mash. Stir in butter. Spoon into a greased 9" pie plate. Spread over bottom and up sides of plate, building up sides to form a crust. Arrange vegetables in bottom of potato crust; sprinkle with cheese.

In a small bowl combine milk, eggs, flour, and seasonings; pour over cheese. Bake for 40 to 50 minutes.

Note: *To save time, use instant mashed potatoes. It takes 1 1/3 cups prepared instant potatoes to equal the potatoes called for.*

Makes 6 servings. Per serving: *265 Calories; 12g Fat; 15g Protein; 21g Carbohydrate; 137mg Cholesterol; 475mg Sodium*

Roasted Garlic on Bruschetta

BY STACEY PEDERSEN

Living in California, we are well exposed to garlic as an ingredient in our cuisine. The state is home to Gilroy, the self-proclaimed "Garlic Capital of the World." We also have restaurants devoted to garlic and called by its nickname, "The Stinking Rose." Pass the breath mints, please!

375°

- 1 bulb garlic
- 3 tablespoons olive oil, divided
- 1 16-ounce French baguette
- Salt
- 2 tablespoons grated Parmesan cheese

Slice garlic bulb in half crosswise; drizzle each half with 1 1/2 teaspoons olive oil. Wrap in foil and bake until soft, about 45 minutes.

To make bruschetta, cut the bread on the diagonal into 1/3"-thick slices. Brush the bread on both sides with 2 tablespoons of olive oil and season lightly with salt. Arrange in a single layer on a baking sheet. Bake about 15 minutes, turning once halfway through. To serve, sprinkle each piece of bread with Parmesan cheese and serve with roasted garlic, spreading garlic on toasted bread.

KALAMATA OLIVE SPREAD *(alternative topping)*

- 1 cup pitted Kalamata olives
- 1 tablespoon olive oil
- 1 clove garlic, minced
- 2 1/2 tablespoons Parmesan cheese

In a food processor, blend all ingredients until well mixed.

Makes 8 servings. Per serving: *118 Calories; 6g Fat; 6g Protein; 34g Carbohydrate; 1mg Cholesterol; 284mg Sodium*

Roasted Potatoes and Broccoli

In our house, we love potatoes in almost every form imaginable. Perhaps that is due, in part, to one of Jim's distant French relatives. Antoine Augustin Parmentier, an agricultural specialist, popularized the potato by introducing it to Louis XVI and Marie Antoinette. What was enjoyed by royalty soon was demanded by everyone.*

- 4 large baking potatoes, unpeeled, cut into wedges
- 2 tablespoons olive oil
- 4 cloves garlic, minced
- 1 teaspoon salt
- 1 pound broccoli, cut into florets, steamed just tender
- 2 tablespoons grated Parmesan cheese

In a large bowl, toss together the potatoes, olive oil, garlic, and salt. Spread on a baking sheet. Bake, turning once or twice, until well browned and crisp, 50 minutes. Add the broccoli to the potatoes. Roast, turning once, 5 to 7 minutes longer. Serve very hot, sprinkled with the cheese.

Makes 6 servings. Per serving: *151 Calories; 5g Fat; 5g Protein; 23g Carbohydrate; 1mg Cholesterol; 413mg Sodium*

Savory Acorn Squash

Acorn squash is a part of the family of winter squash that also includes such varieties as banana, buttercup, butternut, carnival, delicate, golden nugget, hubbard, kabocha, spaghetti, sweet dumpling, turban, and pumpkin. You'll find that this version is not your typical baked squash!

2 acorn squash
1 cube vegetable bouillon
2 tablespoons boiling water
1 egg, slightly beaten, or 1/4 cup Morningstar Farms® *Scramblers®*
2 tablespoons butter, divided
1/4 cup chopped onion
1 1/2 cups crushed seasoned bread stuffing
1/4 cup grated Parmesan cheese
1/2 teaspoon salt
1/4 cup seasoned bread crumbs

Cut squash in half lengthwise; wrap each with plastic wrap and place in microwave-safe dish. Microwave on high 8 1/2 to 11 1/2 minutes, rotating and rearranging after 5 or 6 minutes. Let stand 5 to10 minutes. Remove squash from shells, leaving a 1/4"-thick shell. Mash.

Dissolve bouillon cube in water. Add egg and bouillon to mashed squash.

Sauté onion in 1 tablespoon butter until onion is tender. Mix onion, stuffing mix, Parmesan cheese, and salt into mashed squash. Fill shells with mixture.

Melt 1 tablespoon butter and mix with bread crumbs. Top squash with crumb mixture. Bake for 30 to 40 minutes.

Makes 12 servings. Per serving: *125 Calories; 3g Fat; 4g Protein; 20g Carbohydrate; 24mg Cholesterol; 692mg Sodium*

Scalloped Eggplant

Why are they called eggplants? Because originally the skins were white, which made them look like giant eggs! Thomas Jefferson brought the first eggplants to the United States.*

375°

- 2 medium eggplants
- 2 tablespoons olive oil
- 1 medium yellow onion, chopped, or 1 tablespoon dehydrated onion
- 2 cloves garlic, minced
- 1 teaspoon crushed dried basil
- 1 teaspoon crushed dried oregano
- 1/2 teaspoon salt
- 3 medium fresh tomatoes, peeled, seeded, and chopped
- 1 1/2 cups shredded Swiss cheese

Peel eggplants and cut into 1" cubes. Bring about 1" of lightly salted water to boil in a 2-quart saucepan; add eggplant. Boil for 1 minute; do not overcook. Drain, gently squeeze out excess moisture, and set aside.

Heat oil in saucepan; add onion and garlic; cook, uncovered, over moderate heat for 5 minutes or until translucent. Combine with eggplant, herbs, and salt. Place mixture in a greased 2-quart baking dish. Distribute tomatoes evenly over top. Bake for 30 minutes. Sprinkle with cheese; bake an additional 5 minutes or until cheese melts.

Makes 8 servings. Per serving: *156 Calories; 10g Fat; 8g Protein; 11g Carbohydrate; 20mg Cholesterol; 197mg Sodium*

Chapter 3: 400 Degrees

Entrees

Side Dishes

Asparagus Pockets With Hollandaise

Roman emperors were so fond of asparagus that they kept a special fleet of ships just for the purpose of fetching it! These easy pockets, using this vegetable delicacy, are an elegant and satisfying combination.

- 1 package frozen puff pastry sheets, thawed
- 2 tablespoons butter, melted
- 8 Worthington® Meatless Wham Vegetable Protein Slices
- 8 slices Swiss cheese (about 8 ounces)
- 1 pound fresh or 1 10-ounce package frozen, thawed asparagus spears
- 1 1-ounce package Hollandaise sauce mix

Cut one sheet of puff pastry into 4 squares. Brush lightly with butter. Layer on one square 1 piece of Wham, 1 slice cheese, and one-eighth of the asparagus. Bring pastry around filling, sealing edges well. Repeat with remaining ingredients. Place, seam side down, on a greased baking sheet (be sure sides don't touch). Brush with remaining butter. Bake for 30 minutes or until golden.

Meanwhile, prepare sauce mix according to package directions. Serve over the pockets.

Makes 8 servings. Per serving: *382 Calories; 14g Fat; 18g Protein; 42g Carbohydrate; 34mg Cholesterol; 670mg Sodium*

Baked Reuben Sandwich

The origin of the Reuben sandwich is somewhat clouded in debate between a restaurant in Omaha, Nebraska, and one in New York City. Regardless of where it began, the sandwich consists of rye bread, corned beef, sauerkraut, Swiss cheese, and dressing. We have found this main-dish version of the classic sandwich to be filling and tasty too!

- 2 10-ounce packages refrigerated pizza crust
- 1/2 cup low-fat Thousand Island salad dressing
- 1 8-ounce package Worthington® Meatless Corned Beef Slices, thawed
- 1 16-ounce can sauerkraut, rinsed and drained
- 2 cups shredded or 8 ounces thinly sliced Swiss cheese
- 1 egg white, lightly beaten, or 1/4 cup Egg Beaters® Egg Whites
- 1 tablespoon water
- 1 teaspoon caraway seed (optional)

Unroll 1 pizza crust onto lightly floured surface; roll out to 12" x 9" rectangle. Spread half of the Thousand Island dressing over crust. Cover with half of the beef slices, sauerkraut, and cheese to within 1 inch of long (seam) edge of dough. Starting with the longest edge of rectangle, roll up dough, jelly-roll style; press seam together to seal. Repeat with remaining crust and filling. Place rolls, seam sides down, on greased baking sheet.

In a small bowl, combine egg white and water; brush onto rolls and sprinkle half the caraway seed on each roll. Bake 20 to 25 minutes or until golden brown. Let stand 10 minutes before cutting.

Makes 12 servings. Per serving: *270 Calories; 11g Fat; 13g Protein; 30g Carbohydrate; 19mg Cholesterol; 940mg Sodium*

ALTERNATE TURKEY FILLING:

- 2/3 cup cheddar cheese pasta sauce
- 1 16-ounce bag frozen chopped broccoli, thawed and drained
- 1/2 teaspoon garlic powder
- 1/2 teaspoon onion powder
- 1 teaspoon chickenlike seasoning and broth mix
- 2 10-ounce packages refrigerated pizza crust
- 8 ounces of Worthington® Meatless Smoked Turkey Slices
- 1 egg white, lightly beaten, or 1/4 cup Egg Beaters® Egg Whites
- 1 tablespoon water
- 2 tablespoons grated Parmesan cheese

400°

Combine sauce, broccoli, and seasonings.

Unroll 1 pizza crust onto lightly floured surface; roll out to 12" x 9" rectangle. Place half the turkey slices on the dough; cover with half the broccoli mixture to within 1 inch of long (seam) edge of dough. Start rolling from longest edge of rectangle, jelly-roll style; press seam together to seal. Repeat this process with the remaining dough and filling. Place rolls, seam sides down, on greased baking sheet.

In a small bowl, combine egg white and water; brush onto rolls and sprinkle with Parmesan cheese. Bake 20 to 25 minutes or until golden brown. Let stand 10 minutes before cutting.

HOMEMADE DOUGH *as an alternate to purchased crust (use a bread machine to do the work for you!):*

- 1 1/2 teaspoons dry yeast
- 2 1/3 cups flour
- 1/3 cup semolina or cornmeal
- 2 teaspoons salt
- 2 teaspoons sugar
- 2 tablespoons olive oil
- 1 cup warm (not hot) water

Place ingredients in bread machine in the order recommended. Add flour as needed until dough pulls away from sides of pan. Let dough mix through the dough cycle until the machine stops. Divide dough in half and roll out as directed.

Cauliflower Wham au Gratin

Did you know that you can keep cauliflower white during cooking by adding lemon to the water? Also, one serving of cauliflower contains 100% of your recommended daily amount of vitamin C!

- 4 cups fresh cauliflower florets or 2 10-ounce packages frozen cauliflower, thawed
- 1/2 8-ounce package Worthington® Meatless Wham Vegetable Protein Slices, cubed
- 1 11-ounce can condensed cheddar cheese soup
- 1/4 cup 2% milk
- 1/4 cup buttermilk baking mix
- 2 tablespoons butter
- 2 tablespoons shredded low-fat cheddar cheese
- 1/2 teaspoon ground nutmeg

Arrange cauliflower in a greased 8" x 8" baking dish; sprinkle with Wham.

Mix soup and milk until smooth; pour over Wham.

For topping, cut butter into baking mix. Stir in cheese and nutmeg. Sprinkle over soup mixture. Bake for 30 minutes or until topping is golden brown and cauliflower is tender.

Makes 6 servings. Per serving: *124 Calories; 7g Fat; 4g Protein; 12g Carbohydrate; 16mg Cholesterol; 532mg Sodium*

Cheddar Chicken Potpie

Puff pastry is made by folding layers of butter and dough over and over again. The French term for this pastry, *mille-feuilles,* literally means "1,000 leaves." Here it makes a perfect topping for the savory chicken filling.

400°

1 1/2 cups + 2 teaspoons water, divided
1 1/2 tablespoons chickenlike seasoning and broth mix
1/2 cup frozen peas
1/2 cup thinly sliced carrots
2 celery stalks, thinly sliced
1/2 cup chopped onion or 1 tablespoon dried onion
1/2 cup button mushrooms or quartered regular mushrooms
2 medium red potatoes, cubed small
1/4 cup flour
1 1/2 cups 2% milk
2 cups shredded sharp cheddar cheese
2 13-ounce cans Worthington® Meatless Chicken Diced, drained
1 teaspoon chopped fresh or 1/2 teaspoon dried thyme
1/4 teaspoon poultry seasoning
1/2 teaspoon salt
1/2 package (1 sheet) puff pastry
1 egg or 1/4 cup Morningstar Farms® *Scramblers®*

In a large saucepan, mix together 1 1/2 cups water and chickenlike seasoning; bring to a boil. Add vegetables; simmer 10 to 15 minutes or until tender.

Blend flour with milk; stir into broth mixture. Cook and stir over medium heat until slightly thickened and bubbly. Remove from heat. Add cheese, chicken, and seasonings. Stir to melt cheese. Spoon into a 3-quart casserole.

Cut puff pastry to fit top of dish. Use extra pieces for decorative designs on top. Make several slits in crust to let steam escape. Brush rim of dish with 1 teaspoon water. Place crust on top, pressing edges lightly.

Beat egg with 1 teaspoon water and brush over crust. Bake 40 to 45 minutes or until puffed and golden brown. Let rest 5 minutes before serving.

Makes 8 servings. Per serving: *345 Calories; 12g Fat; 23g Protein; 35g Carbohydrate; 60mg Cholesterol; 1053mg Sodium*

Chicken Wellington

Puff pastry, used in this recipe, "puffs" when baked because the moisture in the butter used to make the dough creates steam between the hundreds of layers, causing them to separate. A pleasing combination of flavors and textures greets the palate with the first bite of this special entree.

1 package frozen puff pastry sheets
1 cup sliced carrots
2 broccoli stalks, sliced
1/4 cup butter
2 12-ounce cans Worthington® *Low Fat FriChik®*, sliced
1 medium onion, chopped, or 1 tablespoon onion powder
1 cup chopped fresh mushrooms
2 packets G. Washington's® Golden Seasoning and Broth
2 teaspoons garlic powder
1 teaspoon cumin seed
1 teaspoon caraway seed
2 8-ounce packages fat-free cream cheese, room temperature
2 eggs or 1/2 cup Morningstar Farms® *Scramblers®*
3/4 cup cracker crumbs
1 egg white, beaten, or 1/2 cup Egg Beaters® *Egg Whites*

Thaw puff pastry according to package directions. Roll out 1 sheet plus 1/3 of second sheet to 1/4" thickness. Line bottom and sides of lightly greased 9" or 10" springform pan, leaving a 1/2" overhang.

Steam carrots and broccoli until crisp-tender. Sauté in butter with *FriChik®*, onion, and mushrooms until tender. Stir in seasonings, cream cheese, eggs, and cracker crumbs. Mix well. Pour filling into pastry-lined pan.

Roll remaining pastry to fit the 9" or 10" top, cut a circle to fit. Place on top of filling. Pull up overhanging pastry to seal to the top and make a fluted edge. Cut air vents and use scraps of pastry to decorate. Brush with egg white. Bake for 50 to 60 minutes or until golden. Remove from oven and cool slightly. Release from pan to serve. Cut with electric knife or thin sharp knife. Serve warm or at room temperature.

Makes 10 servings. Per serving: *352 Calories; 8g Fat; 19g Protein; 47g Carbohydrate; 63mg Cholesterol; 1021 mg Sodium*

Chik and Rice Divan

What's the difference between white and brown rice? White rice is just brown rice that has been polished, no longer having the bran coat and germ. Brown rice is more nutritious than white rice, but takes longer to cook. If you have rice of either color left over from another meal, this is a delicious way to use it up!

- 1 16-ounce package frozen broccoli florets, cooked and drained
- 1/2 cup grated Parmesan cheese, divided
- 1 12.5-ounce can Worthington® Sliced Chik, drained and cubed
- 1 teaspoon salt, divided
- 1 cup cooked rice
- 2 tablespoons butter
- 2 cloves garlic, crushed
- 2 tablespoons flour
- 1 cup 2% milk
- 1 tablespoon lemon juice
- 1 cup light sour cream

Arrange cooked broccoli in a greased 7" x 11" baking dish. Sprinkle with 1/4 cup Parmesan cheese. Top with cubed Sliced Chik and season with 1/2 teaspoon salt. Spread cooked rice over top.

In a medium saucepan, melt butter over low heat. Add garlic and sauté 2 minutes. Blend in flour and 1/2 teaspoon salt. Add milk. Cook over medium heat, stirring constantly until mixture thickens and bubbles. Remove from heat and stir in lemon juice and sour cream. Pour over chicken in casserole. Top with remaining 1/4 cup Parmesan cheese. Bake for 20 to 30 minutes or until browned.

Makes 8 servings. Per serving: *156 Calories; 6g Fat; 11g Protein; 15g Carbohydrate; 16mg Cholesterol; 561mg Sodium*

Choplets Parmigiana

Any of the round vegetarian chops can be used for this recipe, which is our vegetarian version of veal parmigiana. *Parmigiana* simply means "with tomato sauce and cheese."

3 tablespoons butter
1/2 cup Kellogg's® Corn Flake Crumbs
1/4 cup grated Parmesan cheese
1 egg, beaten, or 1/4 cup Morningstar Farms® *Scramblers®*
1 20-ounce can Worthington® *Choplets®*
1 15-ounce can tomato sauce
1 teaspoon crushed dried oregano
1/2 teaspoon sugar
1/2 teaspoon onion powder
8 slices (1 6-ounce package) provolone cheese

Melt butter in 9" x 13" baking dish. Combine Corn Flake Crumbs and Parmesan cheese.

Dip *Choplets®* in egg, then in crumb mixture. Place in baking dish. Bake for 15 minutes; turn *Choplets®* over and bake another 15 minutes.

Meanwhile, in a small saucepan combine tomato sauce, oregano, sugar, and onion powder; heat just to boiling, stirring frequently. Pour sauce over *Choplets®*; top each with a slice of cheese. Return to oven to melt cheese slices, about 3 minutes. Serve with buttered noodles.

Note: *A favorite bottled pasta sauce may be used in place of tomato sauce mixture.*

Makes 8 servings. Per serving: *209 Calories; 12g Fat; 40g Protein; 8g Carbohydrate; 55mg Cholesterol; 840mg Sodium*

Corn-Crusted Chicken Turnovers

Entrees baked inside a crust always provide a surprise. They can be traced back to the days of old England through the nursery rhyme that talks about "four and twenty blackbirds baked in a pie."
Trust us, the only "birds" in these turnovers are made from soy!

- 1 3-ounce package cream cheese, room temperature
- 1 tablespoon 2% milk
- 1 12.5-ounce can Worthington® *Low Fat FriChik®*, finely diced
- 1 cup shredded low-fat cheddar cheese
- 1/4 cup sliced green onions or 1 teaspoon onion powder
- 3 tablespoons diced green chiles
- 1/2 teaspoon garlic salt
- 1/2 teaspoon ground cumin
- 1 17-ounce package grand size refrigerator biscuits
- 2 tablespoons butter, melted
- 1 1/3 cups corn chips (about 6 ounces)

Cream together cream cheese and milk; add *FriChik®*, cheese, onions, chiles, garlic salt, and cumin; set aside.

Roll out each biscuit into a 4" circle. Place 1/4 cup filling on each circle, moisten outer edges. Fold dough to enclose filling. Press edges with a fork to seal. Brush tops with melted butter.

Crush corn chips into fine crumbs; then press buttered side of turnovers into them to coat. Place on an ungreased baking sheet. Bake for 20 minutes or until golden.

Makes 8 servings. Per serving: *383 Calories; 21g Fat; 12g Protein; 32g Carbohydrate; 22mg Cholesterol; 927mg Sodium*

Corned Beef Tamale Pie

A tamale pie is defined as "a dish made with the ingredients of a regular tamale (cornmeal batter, ground meat, cheese, and seasonings), except the ingredients are layered and baked in a dish instead of wrapped in a corn husk." This one is a little different from the expected.

1 1/2 cups yellow cornmeal
3/4 teaspoon salt
1 cup cold water
3 cups boiling water
2 tablespoons vegetable oil
1 medium onion, finely chopped, or 1 tablespoon dried onion
1/2 cup chopped green pepper
1 clove garlic, minced
1 1/2 8-ounce packages Worthington® Meatless Corned Beef Slices, chopped
1 15-ounce can tomato sauce
2 tablespoons chili powder
1/2 teaspoon salt
1/2 teaspoon ground cumin
1 cup shredded low-fat cheddar cheese
1 6-ounce can large, pitted black olives, halved

Mix cornmeal, salt, and cold water in a medium-size saucepan. Add boiling water; bring to a boil. Cook over moderate heat, stirring frequently until mixture is thick, about 3 to 5 minutes. Remove from heat. Cool.

Meanwhile, heat oil in large skillet; sauté onion, green pepper, and garlic until golden and tender, but not brown. Add corned beef, tomato sauce, chili powder, salt, and cumin. Stir over moderate heat until mixture comes to a boil. Remove from heat; add cheese and olives; stir until cheese is melted.

Line the sides, but not the bottom, of a greased 2-quart casserole with 3/4 of the cornmeal mixture by placing mixture around sides and using the back of a large spoon to scrape and press it up the sides to the rim. Spoon corned beef mixture into center of casserole; spread remaining cornmeal around edges on top of casserole, leaving a 2- to 3-inch opening at the center. Using a wet spatula, spread cornmeal smoothly over top and toward edges of casserole, sealing completely. Bake for 60 minutes or until lightly browned on top and bubbling in the middle. Let stand 15 minutes before serving.

Makes 8 servings. Per serving: *332 Calories; 15g Fat; 14g Protein; 31g Carbohydrate; 3mg Cholesterol; 1357mg Sodium*

Greek Chicken and Manestra

BY BILL PAPPAS

Debi grew up eating this with "the real thing." She's taken the traditional recipe and adapted it into a vegetarian dish, so when she's hungry for that certain taste, it's there!

- 1 1/2 cups orzo pasta
- 1 15-ounce can tomato sauce
- 1 3/4 cups water
- 1 tablespoon olive oil
- 1 teaspoon chickenlike seasoning and broth mix
- 1 tablespoon crushed dried oregano
- 2 tablespoons butter, cut up
- 2 cloves garlic, crushed
- 2 12-ounce cans Worthington® *Low Fat FriChik®*, drained and halved

Mix together orzo, tomato sauce, water, olive oil, seasonings, butter, and garlic in 2-quart casserole. Place *FriChik®* pieces into pasta. Bake for 15 minutes. Remove from oven, gently stir, and return to oven for 15 more minutes. Remove from oven, gently stir, and return to oven. Bake 15 minutes more or until pasta is soft and most of the liquid is absorbed.

Note: *Make and bake this the same day!*

Makes 8 servings. Per serving: *170 Calories; 7g Fat; 8g Protein; 17g Carbohydrate; 8mg Cholesterol; 664mg Sodium*

Mother's Stuffed Cabbage

BY PATRICIA ROSE

This was one of the favorite family dinners at Debi's house. Usually it was the only dish served so that the family could just eat their fill of cabbage rolls.

- 1 large cabbage (about 3 1/2 pounds)
- 1 1-ounce package Morningstar Farms™ *Ground Meatless®* Crumbles, thawed
- 1 medium onion, chopped, or 1 tablespoon onion powder
- 2 cups cooked rice
- 2 eggs or 1/2 cup Morningstar Farms® *Scramblers®*
- 1/2 teaspoon salt
- 1/2 teaspoon garlic powder
- 1 teaspoon poultry seasoning
- 1 tablespoon flour
- 2 10-ounce cans condensed low-fat tomato soup
- 3/4 cup brown sugar
- 1 cup water

Separate cabbage leaves from head and microwave for 2 minutes at a time to soften. Cut large leaves in half and remove hard stem.

For filling, mix Crumbles, onion, rice, eggs, seasonings, and flour. Place 2 to 3 tablespoons of filling (depending on leaf size) on one edge of each leaf and roll up to enclose filling. If needed, use toothpicks to secure. Lay cabbage rolls in a greased 9" x 13" baking dish, squeezing them in so they all fit. Spoon undiluted tomato soup over rolls, sprinkle with brown sugar, and pour on water. Cover, set on a cookie sheet, and bake for 90 minutes.

Makes 10 servings. Per serving: *230 Calories; 2g Fat; 12g Protein; 41g Carbohydrate; 43mg Cholesterol; 629mg Sodium*

Sesame Baked Dinner Cuts

The single largest purchaser of sesame seeds in the United States is a certain hamburger chain that features golden arches! But sesame seeds were known back in biblical days and were used to produce oil, not to be the topping for burger buns!

400°

- 1/4 cup oil, divided
- 1/2 teaspoon dried basil
- 2 tablespoons lemon juice
- 1/4 cup breading meal
- 1/3 cup brewer's yeast flakes
- 1/4 cup sesame seeds, untoasted
- 1 20-ounce can Loma Linda® Dinner Cuts, drained

Use 1 tablespoon oil to grease a baking sheet.

Mix together 3 tablespoons oil, basil, and lemon juice.

In separate bowl, stir together breading meal, yeast flakes, and sesame seeds.

Dip Dinner Cuts into oil mixture and then into breading meal. Place on an oiled baking sheet. Bake for 10 minutes. Turn Dinner Cuts over and bake an additional 10 minutes or until brown. Serve with favorite gravy.

Makes 8 servings. Per serving: *158 Calories; 10g Fat; 13g Protein; 6g Carbohydrate; 0mg Cholesterol; 254mg Sodium*

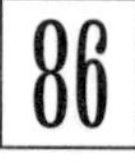

Smitty's Meatless Meatloaf

As we understand it, Smitty was a cookware salesman many years ago who developed this vegetarian recipe to help sell the product. It "sold" us on a new form of an old favorite!

- 3 eggs, beaten, or 3/4 cup Morningstar Farms® *Scramblers®*
- 1 20-ounce can Worthington® Low Fat Vegetarian Burger
- 2 cups raw rolled oats
- 1 large onion, grated, or 1 tablespoon dehydrated onion
- 1 cup shredded carrots
- 1 medium potato, grated
- 1 cup shredded low-fat cheddar cheese
- 1 15-ounce can creamed corn
- 1 16-ounce can stewed tomatoes, broken up
- 1/4 cup vegetable oil
- 2 teaspoons (rounded) ground sage
- 2 teaspoons salt

400°

Mix together all ingredients thoroughly and place in a greased 9" x 13" baking dish. Bake for 50 to 60 minutes.

Makes 12 servings. Per serving: *236 Calories; 9g Fat; 15g Protein; 22g Carbohydrate; 55mg Cholesterol; 899mg Sodium*

Spinach Meatballs

Meatballs don't have to be fried to be good. Using spinach in them also significantly increases the nutritional value. Adding the sauce after baking helps the balls hold together.

- 1 10-ounce package frozen chopped spinach, thawed and drained
- 1 medium onion, finely chopped, or 1 tablespoon onion powder
- 1 clove garlic, minced
- 1 20-ounce can Worthington® Low Fat Vegetarian Burger
- 6 tablespoons grated Parmesan cheese, divided
- 3 tablespoons bread crumbs
- 1 egg, beaten, or 1/4 cup Morningstar Farms® *Scramblers®*
- 1 teaspoon salt
- 2 tablespoons butter
- 2 tablespoons flour
- 1 8-ounce can tomato sauce
- 1 cup water (or liquid from vegetables)

Combine spinach, onion, garlic, and burger; add 3 tablespoons Parmesan cheese; add bread crumbs, egg, and salt and mix well. Press into balls about the size of golf balls. Place in greased 7" x 11" baking dish. Bake for 30 to 40 minutes.

Make sauce by melting butter in medium sauce pan; remove from heat and stir in flour. Gradually stir in tomato sauce and water. Cook, stirring, until thickened. Pour sauce over hot meatballs. Sprinkle top with 3 tablespoons Parmesan cheese.

Makes 8 servings. Per serving: *165 Calories; 7g Fat; 16g Protein; 10g Carbohydrate; 37mg Cholesterol; 968mg Sodium*

Tallerine

BY PATRICIA ROSE

Speaking of easy and quick to prepare, this dish is a winner in taste and family appeal. Do you wonder what the unique, international-sounding name means? So do we!

- 1 tablespoon vegetable oil
- 1 20-ounce can Worthington® Low Fat Vegetarian Burger
- 1 small onion, chopped fine, or 1 tablespoon onion powder
- 1 14.5-ounce can diced tomatoes
- 1 15-ounce can creamed corn
- 1/2 cup water
- 2 cups uncooked noodles
- 1/2 teaspoon salt
- 2 cloves garlic, crushed
- 1 cup shredded low-fat cheddar cheese

In a large skillet, sauté burger and onion in oil. Add rest of ingredients except cheese and mix well. Place mixture in a greased 9" x 13" baking dish. Top with cheese. Cover and bake for 30 minutes. Remove cover and bake 15 minutes longer.

Makes 10 servings. Per serving: *175 Calories; 5g Fat; 14g Protein; 17g Carbohydrate; 10mg Cholesterol; 730mg Sodium*

Western Beef and Corn Casserole

Think of this as an upside-down tamale pie—barbeque style. Since tamale pie, which became popular in the U.S. during the mid 1920s, can contain almost anything you want, why not try it this way?

- 1 tablespoon vegetable oil
- 1 16-ounce package Morningstar Farms™ *Ground Meatless®* Crumbles, thawed
- 1/2 teaspoon chili powder
- 2 cups shredded low-fat cheddar cheese, divided
- 1/2 cup hickory or regular barbecue sauce
- 1 11-ounce can Mexican-style corn, drained
- 1 8-ounce can tomato sauce
- 1 cup flour
- 1/2 cup yellow cornmeal
- 2 tablespoons sugar
- 1 teaspoon salt
- 1 teaspoon baking powder
- 1/4 cup butter
- 1/2 cup 2% milk
- 1 egg, beaten, or 1/4 cup Morningstar Farms® *Scramblers®*

Brown the burger in oil. Stir in chili powder, 1 cup shredded cheese, barbecue sauce, corn, and tomato sauce; set aside.

To make the crust, stir together flour, cornmeal, sugar, salt, and baking powder; cut in butter. Blend in milk, egg, and 1/2 cup cheese. Spread crust mixture over the bottom of a greased 8" x 8" baking pan. Pour filling over crust. Sprinkle with remaining 1/2 cup cheese. Bake for 25 to 30 minutes.

Makes 8 servings. Per serving: *370 Calories; 11g Fat; 22g Protein; 38g Carbohydrate; 49mg Cholesterol; 1217mg Sodium*

Artichoke Torte

Did you know that artichokes are part of the sunflower family? Ninety-eight percent of the world's artichokes grow in California. This unique vegetable is spotlighted here in a smooth custard filling.

- 8 eggs or 2 cups Morningstar Farms® *Scramblers®*
- 3 tablespoons pesto
- 1 teaspoon garlic powder
- 2 teaspoons Italian herb seasoning
- 1 cup plain bread crumbs
- 1/2 cup finely chopped onion or 1 tablespoon onion powder
- 1 cup grated Parmesan cheese
- 2 13-ounce cans artichoke hearts, drained and cut small

In a large mixing bowl, beat the eggs. Add the pesto, garlic powder, and Italian seasoning; stir. Add the bread crumbs, onion, and Parmesan cheese; stir. Fold in the artichoke hearts and pour into a greased 8" x 8" baking dish. Bake until lightly brown on the outside, 40 to 45 minutes.

Makes 8 servings. Per serving: *236 Calories; 12g Fat; 15g Protein; 17g Carbohydrate; 222mg Cholesterol; 630mg Sodium*

Cauliflower and Mushroom Gougere

A *gougere* is a pastry and vegetable dish that originated in the Burgundy region of France. Here, a cheesy cream puff encircles the tasty filling, making this a spectacular presentation.

- 1 1/4 cups water
- 1/2 cup + 1 tablespoon butter, divided
- 1 1/2 cups all-purpose flour
- 4 eggs or 1 cup Morningstar Farms® *Scramblers®*
- 1 cup shredded Gruyère or cheddar cheese
- 1 teaspoon salt, divided
- 1 tablespoon oil
- 1 small onion, finely chopped, or 1 tablespoon onion powder
- 4 ounces mushrooms, halved if large
- 3 cups cauliflower florets
- 1 14-ounce can diced tomatoes with roasted garlic
- 1/2 teaspoon chopped fresh thyme

Place the water and 1/2 cup butter in a large saucepan and heat until the butter has melted. Remove from the heat and add all the flour at once. Beat well with a large spoon for about 30 seconds until smooth. Allow to cool slightly. Beat in the eggs, one at a time, and continue beating until the mixture is thick and glossy. Stir in the cheese and 1/2 teaspoon salt. Spread the mixture around the sides of a greased 7" x 11" baking dish, leaving a hollow in the center for the filling.

To make the filling, heat the oil and 1 tablespoon butter in a medium skillet and sauté the onion for 3 to 4 minutes, until softened but not browned. Add the mushrooms and cook for 2 to 3 minutes, until they begin to be flecked with brown. Add the cauliflower and stir-fry for 1 minute.

Purée the tomatoes in a blender or food processor; add the thyme and remaining 1/2 teaspoon salt; pour mixture into the vegetables. Cook, uncovered, over low heat for about 5 minutes until the cauliflower is only just tender. Spoon the mixture into the hollow in the baking dish, adding all the liquid. Bake for 40 to 50 minutes, until the outer pastry is well risen and golden brown.

Makes 8 servings. Per serving: *338 Calories; 22g Fat; 12g Protein; 24g Carbohydrate; 156mg Cholesterol; 662mg Sodium*

Creamy Broccoli

Former U.S. President George Bush said: "I do not like broccoli. And I haven't liked it since I was a little kid and my mother made me eat it. And I'm President of the United States and I'm not going to eat any more broccoli." His plane, Air Force One, was even declared a "Broccoli-Free Zone!"* Perhaps he never tried it in this creamy form.

- 2 16-ounce packages frozen chopped broccoli, thawed and pressed dry
- 1 10.5-ounce can condensed low-fat cream of celery soup
- 1 cup low-fat cottage cheese
- 2 eggs, well beaten, or 1/2 cup Morningstar Farms® *Scramblers®*
- 1 cup shredded low-fat cheddar cheese
- 1/2 cup light mayonnaise
- 1/2 cup light sour cream
- 2 tablespoons chopped onion or 1/2 teaspoon onion powder
- 1 teaspoon Vege-Sal® seasoning
- 1/2 cup ranch-style sliced almond salad topping

Combine broccoli, celery soup, cottage cheese, eggs, cheese, mayonaise, sour cream, onion, and seasoning. Place in greased 7" x 11" baking dish. Sprinkle with almonds. Bake for 40 to 50 minutes or until firm.

Makes 8 servings. Per serving: *196 Calories; 7g Fat; 13g Protein; 13g Carbohydrate; 67mg Cholesterol; 585mg Sodium*

Easy Cheese Souffle

BY PATRICIA ROSE

James Beard, world-famous chef, is quoted as saying, "The only thing that will make a souffle fall is if it knows you are afraid of it!"* Debi's mother was an accomplished cook who had an eye for delicious, yet easy, recipes. This is one of her "finds."

400°

- 1 cup 2% milk, scalded
- 1 cup white bread cubes, crusts removed
- 1 cup shredded low-fat cheddar cheese
- 1 tablespoon butter
- 1/2 teaspoon salt
- 3 eggs

In a medium bowl, pour hot milk over bread, cheese, butter, and salt. Stir to melt butter and cheese. Let cool. Separate eggs. Beat yolks and add to cooled milk mixture. Whip whites until peaks form, but not too stiff, and fold into milk. Pour into a greased 8" x 8" baking dish. Bake for 20 minutes or until knife comes out clean.

Makes 6 servings. Per serving: *202 Calories; 7g Fat; 11g Protein; 18g Carbohydrate; 119mg Cholesterol; 682mg Sodium*

French Rice and Spinach Tian

The name of this dish comes from the earthenware dish in which it is cooked in Provence. And, yes, you read correctly! The spinach stems are chopped and used also. Brown rice gives a chewy quality to this dish.

- 1 cup brown rice
- 2 cups water
- 1 teaspoon salt, divided
- 1 pound fresh spinach
- 1/4 cup olive oil, divided
- 3 cloves garlic, crushed
- 1 tablespoon chopped fresh parsley
- 1 cup shredded low-fat Monterey Jack cheese
- 2 eggs or 1/2 cup Morningstar Farms® *Scramblers®*
- 2 tablespoons dry bread crumbs
- 2 tablespoons grated Parmesan cheese

400°

Wash the rice and put it into a medium saucepan with the water and 1/2 teaspoon of salt. Bring it to a boil; then turn the heat down to the lowest setting and leave the rice to cook, covered, for 40 to 45 minutes, until it's tender and all the liquid has been absorbed. (If there's still some water left in the saucepan, just let it stand off the heat with the lid on for 10 to 15 minutes.)

Wash the spinach thoroughly in three changes of water, then chop it—you can use the stems too. Heat 2 tablespoons olive oil in a large saucepan and put in the spinach, turning it in the hot oil for 2 to 3 minutes until it has softened slightly and looks glossy. Take it off the heat and add the rice, garlic, parsley, and Monterey Jack cheese. Beat in the eggs and 1/2 teaspoon salt and mix well. Spoon the mixture into an 8" x 8" baking dish and sprinkle the crumbs, Parmesan cheese, and the remaining 2 tablespoons olive oil on top. Bake for 30 to 40 minutes, or until it's golden brown and crispy on top.

Note: *Swiss chard can be used in place of spinach. The tian can be served hot or cold.*

Makes 8 servings. Per serving: *249 Calories; 12g Fat; 11g Protein; 25g Carbohydrate; 154mg Cholesterol; 512mg Sodium*

Herb-Roasted Sweet Potatoes

Did you know that Vardaman, Mississippi, claims to be the Sweet Potato Capital of the World, and North Carolina is the largest producer of sweet potatoes in the U.S.?* This recipe is a change from the usual "sweet" potato preparations. And it's so easy too!

400°

- 3 pounds raw sweet potatoes, peeled and cut into 1/2" rounds
- 2 tablespoons crushed fresh thyme leaves or 2 teaspoons dried thyme
- 3 tablespoons olive oil
- 2 teaspoons salt
- 1/2 teaspoon red pepper flakes
- 4 cloves garlic, minced

In a medium bowl, toss sweet potatoes with remaining ingredients. Place in a single layer on baking sheet. Bake for 15 minutes. Remove from oven, turn slices over, and bake 15 more minutes or until sweet potatoes are tender and browned.

Makes 8 servings. Per serving: *228 Calories; 6g Fat; 3g Protein: 42g Carbohydrate; 0mg Cholesterol; 556mg Sodium*

Oven-Fried Asparagus

This graceful vegetable has always been a sign of elegance and often was a delicacy only the wealthy could afford. "As quick as cooking asparagus" was an old Roman saying, which meant that something was accomplished rapidly. This version comes together rather quickly too.

- 1/3 cup plain bread crumbs
- 1 tablespoon grated Parmesan cheese
- 1/4 teaspoon Vege-Sal® seasoning
- 1/4 teaspoon salt
- 2 pounds fresh asparagus, trimmed and cut to the same length
- 2 tablespoons olive oil

Place the bread crumbs, cheese, Vege-Sal® seasoning, and salt in a large plastic bag.

In a large bowl, toss the asparagus with the oil and place the spears in the bag of crumbs. Shake to coat. Arrange the coated asparagus in a single layer on a greased baking sheet. Bake until the coating is browned and crisp, about 30 minutes.

Makes 6 servings. Per serving: *102 Calories; 5g Fat; 4g Protein; 11g Carbohydrate; 1mg Cholesterol; 163mg Sodium*

Sig. 04—M.E.O.C.

Parmesan Potato Wedges

Frederick the Great once ordered his people to plant and eat potatoes as a deterrent to famine in the land. He threatened to cut off the nose and ears of those who refused! No threats here. But if you'd like to cut back on fat and calories, we found these wedges to be just as tasty as if we'd used oil.

2/3 cup plain bread crumbs
1/2 cup grated Parmesan cheese
1 1/2 tablespoons dried oregano or Italian herbs
1/2 teaspoon garlic powder
8 medium potatoes, peeled or unpeeled
Butter-flavor cooking spray
1 teaspoon salt

Combine bread crumbs, Parmesan cheese, oregano, and garlic powder in large bowl.

Scrub or peel potatoes. Cut each potato lengthwise into 12 wedges. Spray generously with butter-flavored cooking spray, tossing and respraying until well coated. Sprinkle salt over potatoes and stir to mix well. Pour bread crumb mixture over top and toss till evenly coated. Place on greased baking sheet. Bake until browned and tender, about 35 minutes, stirring once if desired.

ALTERNATE COATINGS: *The directions are the same.*

SPICY BBQ
1 teaspoon chili powder
1 1/2 teaspoon onion powder
1 1/2 teaspoon garlic powder
1 teaspoon paprika
1 teaspoon sugar

ITALIAN
Olive-oil spray
1/4 cup crushed garlic
1 tablespoon dried rosemary, basil, and/or oregano

Makes 8 servings. Per serving: *151 Calories; 2g Fat; 6g Protein; 28g Carbohydrate; 4mg Cholesterol; 429mg Sodium*

Pesto-Stuffed Mushrooms

We hope that you don't agree with the person who said, "Life is too short to stuff a mushroom."* These mushrooms could double as an appetizer if you wish, but we think they are a yummy side dish! Have you figured out yet that we like pesto?

24 large fresh mushrooms, stems removed and chopped, caps left whole
2 tablespoons olive oil
1/2 cup prepared or homemade pesto
2 tablespoons grated Parmesan cheese

Rub the tops of the mushroom caps with olive oil.

In a medium-size bowl, stir together 1/2 cup chopped mushroom stems and the pesto. Spoon this mixture into the mushroom caps, mounding it a bit in the center. Arrange the filled caps in a single layer in a 7" x 11" baking pan. Sprinkle each with a little cheese. Bake for 15 to 20 minutes or until hot and bubbling. Remove the pan from the oven and cool for several minutes before removing the mushrooms.

Makes 8 servings. Per serving: *125 Calories; 11g Fat; 4g Protein; 4g Carbohydrate; 5mg Cholesterol; 129mg Sodium*

Pine Nut Rissole

The Roman legions are thought to have carried pine nuts as provisions on their conquests through Europe. They are widely used in Mediterranean cooking.

1 tablespoon butter
1/2 cup finely chopped onion
1/4 cup finely chopped celery
1 1/3 cups pine nuts
1/4 cup chopped fresh parsley
2 1/4 cups cooked rice
1 egg or 1/4 cup Morningstar Farms® *Scramblers®*
1 teaspoon Vegex® yeast paste
1/2 teaspoon ground sage
1/2 teaspoon Bakon Seasoning®
2 teaspoons salt, divided
1/2 teaspoon garlic powder
2 cups flour
2/3 cup vegetable shortening
5 tablespoons ice water (may need as many as 7 tablespoons)
2 tablespoons olive oil

Sauté onion and celery in butter.

Toast pine nuts at 300°F approximately 10 to 15 minutes, until slightly golden.

Combine sautéed vegetables, pine nuts, parsley, rice, egg, yeast paste, sage, Bakon Seasoning®, 1/2 teaspoon salt, and garlic powder. Mix well.

For pastry, mix flour and remaining 1 1/2 teaspoons salt. Cut in shortening with pastry blender. Add ice water 1 tablespoon at a time, stirring and pressing together with a fork until dough forms a ball. Divide dough in half. Roll out half of dough into an 8" x 12" rectangle. Place half of pine-nut mixture down center of dough, lengthwise. Moisten one long edge. Fold pastry to center, overlapping slightly and pressing gently together to seal. Transfer carefully to greased baking sheet, placing seam side down. Cut into 2" pieces. Repeat steps with remaining dough and filling. Brush pastry with olive oil. Bake for 30 to 40 minutes or until golden brown. Serve with favorite gravy.

Makes 10 servings. Per serving: *432 Calories; 29g Fat; 10g Protein; 36g Carbohydrate; 32mg Cholesterol; 476mg Sodium*

Puff Spinach Pinwheels

Puff pastry is often used in classic French pastries to create an impressive and crisp dessert. Here it is used for a unique side dish. This recipe goes together in minutes, yet looks like it took hours. Our kind of recipe!

1 package frozen puff pastry sheets, thawed
1 egg, well beaten, or 1/4 cup Morningstar Farms® *Scramblers*®
1 tablespoon water
2 10-ounce packages frozen chopped spinach, thawed, squeezed dry
1 cup shredded low-fat Monterey Jack cheese
1/2 cup grated Parmesan cheese
2 scallions, chopped with tops, or 1/2 teaspoon onion powder
1/4 teaspoon garlic powder
1/2 teaspoon salt
1/4 teaspoon hot pepper sauce
1/2 cup chopped pecans

Place one opened sheet of puffed pastry on a lightly floured board.

Beat egg and water together; brush one side of pastry with the egg mixture, taking care to heavily coat all the edges.

In a bowl, combine remaining ingredients; mix very well. Spread half of the spinach mixture over the entire surface of the open pastry sheet. On the longest side, begin to roll the pastry jelly-roll style; place the seam edge down. Slice the roll into 6 equal pinwheels. Place the pinwheels upright on a greased baking sheet. Repeat entire process with remaining ingredients. Brush the tops with the remaining egg wash. Bake for 20 minutes or until golden.

Makes 12 servings. Per serving: *214 Calories; 7g Fat; 9g Protein; 27g Carbohydrate; 87mg Cholesterol; 452mg Sodium*

Sliced Baked Potatoes

Potatoes became a standard supply item on Spanish exploration ships. It was discovered that sailors who ate them did not suffer from scurvy! The presentation of these vitamin-packed vegetables is unique and attractive. Choose portion-size potatoes for easy serving.

8 medium potatoes
2 teaspoons salt
1/4 cup butter, melted
2 tablespoons chopped fresh
  or 2 teaspoons dried parsley
1 tablespoon chopped fresh or
  1 teaspoon dried thyme
1 tablespoon chopped fresh
  or 1 teaspoon dried chives
1/2 cup shredded low-fat cheddar cheese
3 tablespoons grated Parmesan cheese

Peel potatoes if the skin is tough; otherwise simply scrub and rinse them. Cut potatoes into thin slices, but not all the way through so that the potato stays intact (use a handle of a spoon at the base to prevent the knife from cutting all the way through). Put potatoes in a baking dish; fan them slightly. Sprinkle with salt and drizzle with butter. Sprinkle with herbs. Bake for about 60 minutes. Remove from oven. Sprinkle with cheeses. Bake potatoes for another 10 to 15 minutes until lightly browned, cheeses are melted, and potatoes are soft inside.

Note: *Use caraway seeds or cumin in place of herbs, if desired (use about 3 teaspoons for 8 potatoes). Also, you may use sprigs of fresh herbs instead of chopped herbs.*

Makes 8 servings. Per serving: *168 Calories; 7g Fat; 5g Protein; 21g Carbohydrate; 18mg Cholesterol; 676mg Sodium*

Southern Spoon Bread

BY BERTHA PARMENTIER

Jim has fond memories of eating this dish at the home of his grandmother and great-grandmother. It was often served with warm applesauce as the simple main dish at suppertime. It also makes an elegant side dish to accompany a main meal.

- 2 1/2 cups water
- 1/2 teaspoon salt
- 3 eggs, separated
- 1 cup buttermilk or milk
- 1 cup cornmeal
- 1 teaspoon sugar
- 4 tablespoons butter

Place the water and salt into a 2 1/2- or 3-quart saucepan; bring to a boil.

While the water is heating, whisk together the egg yolks and buttermilk until creamy.

In another bowl, beat the egg whites until stiff.

When the water begins to boil, slowly pour in the cornmeal, using a whisk and stirring briskly to avoid lumps. Add sugar. Whisk for a minute; the cornmeal should be smooth and blended. Remove from heat. Whisk in butter until melted. Slowly stir in the egg-buttermilk mixture. Gently fold in the egg whites. Pour into a greased 8" x 8" baking dish. Bake for 30 to 35 minutes. Serve hot with butter and warm applesauce, if desired.

Makes 6 servings. Per serving: *208 Calories; 11g Fat; 7g Protein; 21g Carbohydrate; 128mg Cholesterol; 333mg Sodium*

Spinach Potato Gratin

Potatoes, which are members of the nightshade family, are the most popular vegetable in the United States. The average American eats about 126 pounds of them a year! Adding spinach to them in this recipe makes for a vitamin-packed meal.

- 3 large baking potatoes
- 4 teaspoons chickenlike seasoning and broth mix
- 1 tablespoon olive oil
- 1/2 pound fresh mushrooms, stems trimmed, thinly sliced
- 1 small onion, thinly sliced, or 2 teaspoons onion powder
- 1 10-ounce package frozen chopped spinach, thawed and squeezed dry
- 3 tablespoons pine nuts
- 2 cloves garlic, minced
- 1 cup low-fat ricotta cheese
- 1 cup light sour cream
- 1 1/2 cups shredded low-fat Monterey Jack cheese
- 1 teaspoon salt
- 1/4 cup grated Parmesan cheese

Peel potatoes and place in a 3-quart saucepan. Add 1 quart water and chicken seasoning. Bring to a soft boil and cook until just tender, about 20 minutes. Drain and thinly slice.

In a small skillet, sauté mushrooms in olive oil over medium heat just until they begin to brown, 6 to 7 minutes.

In a greased 7" x 11" baking dish, spread half the potato slices. Sprinkle the onions over potatoes. Top with spinach, then the mushrooms. Sprinkle with pine nuts.

In a medium bowl beat together the garlic, ricotta, sour cream, Monterey Jack cheese, and salt. Spread half the mixture over the casserole. Top with remaining potatoes, then the rest of the sauce. Sprinkle with Parmesan cheese. Cover and bake for 30 minutes. Remove foil and bake about 15 minutes more until golden brown and bubbling.

Makes 10 servings. Per serving: *178 Calories; 9g Fat; 10g Protein; 15g Carbohydrate; 129mg Cholesterol; 674mg Sodium*

Summer's Bounty Casserole

Advice from about 450 years ago suggested that "a thriving household depends on the use of seasonal produce and the application of common sense."* The message is still true. So when your garden is at its peak, it's just common sense that this dish will make good use of the "fruit of your labor."

- 1 large eggplant, peeled and diced (about 6 cups)
- 4 medium zucchini, sliced
- 1 tablespoon salt, divided
- 3 medium fresh tomatoes, chopped
- 2 medium bell peppers, chopped
- 1 1/2 cups fresh or canned whole-kernel corn
- 1 medium onion, chopped, or 1 tablespoon onion powder
- 1 1/2 cups cooked rice
- 3 tablespoons chopped parsley
- 2 cloves garlic, crushed
- 1/3 cup butter, melted
- 2/3 cup grated Parmesan cheese

Place eggplant and zucchini in a colander. Sprinkle with 1 1/2 teaspoons salt. Let stand for 30 minutes, allowing juices to drain.

In a greased 9" x 13" baking dish, combine eggplant, zucchini, remaining vegetables, rice, parsley, and garlic. Sprinkle with remaining 1 1/2 teaspoons salt. Pour melted butter evenly over vegetables. Cover and bake for 35 minutes. Uncover, sprinkle with Parmesan cheese, and bake 10 to 12 minutes longer or until cheese is melted and vegetables are tender.

Makes 12 servings. Per serving: *151 Calories; 7g Fat; 5g Protein; 19g Carbohydrate; 17mg Cholesterol; 721mg Sodium*

Swiss Cheese Green Beans

Do you know why there are holes in Swiss cheese? As the cheese ferments, gas is produced. As the gas is released, it bubbles through the cheese, leaving all the holes. The humble green bean takes on a new flair with Swiss cheese in this delicious dish. The cereal adds texture and nutrition.

400°

- 2 tablespoons butter
- 2 tablespoons flour
- 1 1/2 cups light sour cream
- 1/2 teaspoon onion powder
- 1 teaspoon salt
- 1/4 teaspoon sugar
- 4 cups frozen green beans, thawed, drained
- 2 cups shredded Swiss cheese
- 3 cups Kellogg's® *Product 19®* cereal

Make a white sauce by melting butter in a 3-quart saucepan. Whisk in flour thoroughly, then sour cream. Heat until it begins to thicken. Add onion powder, salt, and sugar. Add green beans, cheese, and cereal; mix well. Turn into greased 8" x 8" baking dish. Bake for 20 to 30 minutes or until cheese is melted.

Makes 6 servings. Per serving: *284 Calories; 16g Fat; 15g Protein; 24g Carbohydrate; 49mg Cholesterol; 614mg Sodium*

Chapter 4: Make-Ahead Dishes

Breads

Salads & Side Dishes

Desserts

Artichoke Garlic Bread

Did you know that the city of Chicago got its name from the Native American name for the wild garlic that grew around Lake Michigan—*chicagaoua*?* Garlic blends very well with the artichokes and other ingredients in this tasty and easy-to-make bread.

- 1 loaf frozen white-bread dough, thawed
- 1 6-ounce jar marinated artichoke hearts, drained (save the marinade), chopped
- 4 cloves garlic, minced
- 1 cup shredded low-fat Monterey Jack cheese
- 1/2 cup grated Parmesan cheese, divided

On a lightly floured surface, roll dough into a 10" x 12" rectangle. Brush dough with 1 tablespoon artichoke marinade. Evenly top dough with artichokes, garlic, Jack cheese, and Parmesan cheese (reserve 2 tablespoons for topping). From 12" side, lightly roll dough in jelly-roll style. Seal seams. Place roll, seam side down, on baking sheet. Join ends together to form one large ring. With kitchen scissors or sharp knife, cut dough from outside edge of ring to within 1" of inside edge, making cuts every inch. Turn each section on its side so filling shows. Brush dough with half of the remaining marinade and sprinkle with 2 tablespoons of Parmesan cheese. Let dough rise until puffy, 30 to 60 minutes. Bake at 350°F for 20 to 25 minutes or until golden brown. Remove from oven and brush again with marinade. Serve warm.

Makes 16 servings. Per serving: *123 Calories; 5g Fat; 5g Protein; 16g Carbohydrate; 52mg Cholesterol; 270mg Sodium*

Garlicky Spiral Rolls

Caramel pecan rolls are one of Debi's specialties. One day she got the bright idea to copy rolls we'd had at a restaurant and created these savory rolls that are garlicky instead of sweet. They are terrific served warm with an Italian meal.

2 teaspoons active dry yeast
4 cups bread flour
1 tablespoon sugar
1 teaspoon salt
2 cloves garlic, minced
5 tablespoons olive oil, divided
1 1/3 cups water
1 egg or 1/4 cup Morningstar Farms® *Scramblers*®
1/3 cup minced garlic
1/4 cup grated Parmesan cheese

Make-Ahead

Place yeast, flour, sugar, salt, 2 cloves minced garlic, 2 tablespoons olive oil, water, and egg into a bread machine in the order directed by the manufacturer. Remove the dough from the machine at the end of the dough cycle.

Meanwhile, in a small saucepan, lightly sauté 1/3 cup minced garlic in 3 tablespoons olive oil.

Roll the dough into a large rectangle on a floured surface. Spread the sauted garlic and oil completely over the dough. Sprinkle evenly with Parmesan cheese. With a sharp knife, divide the dough in half lengthwise; then roll each side to the center as for a sweet roll. Cut each roll into 12 spirals and place cut side down in a greased 10" x 15" baking dish. Cover and allow to rise until double in size. Bake at 350°F for 20 minutes.

Makes 24 servings. Per serving: *118 Calories; 4g Fat; 3g Protein; 18g Carbohydrate; 10mg Cholesterol; 108mg Sodium*

Restaurant-Style Focaccia

Focaccia is a flat bread with herbs and other seasonings sprinkled across the top.
Many restaurants and bistros are serving this delightful treat.
Our single-rise version is quick, easy, and tasty!

1 package active dry yeast
1 cup warm (100°F) water
1/3 cup olive oil, divided
1 teaspoon honey
3/4 teaspoon salt
1/4 cup grated Parmesan cheese
1/4 cup cold water
3 cups flour
1 teaspoon crushed garlic
1 tablespoon chopped fresh thyme
or rosemary

Dissolve yeast in warm water. Add 1 tablespoon olive oil, honey, salt, Parmesan cheese, cold water, and flour. Mix well.

Combine remaining olive oil and crushed garlic in small bowl.

Grease a baking sheet with additional olive oil.

On lightly floured surface roll out dough with rolling pin to a large rectangle to fit pan and transfer to baking sheet. Make indentations over the dough with fingers and coat top of dough with garlic–olive oil mixture. Sprinkle with thyme or rosemary. Let dough rise about 30 minutes. Bake at 400°F for 25 minutes or until evenly browned. Cool 30 minutes before serving.

Note: *The mixing can be done in a bread machine, adding ingredients in the order suggested by the manufacturer, or in a a heavy-duty mixer using the dough hook attachment.*

Makes 8 servings. Per serving: *270 Calories; l0g Fat; 7g Protein; 37g Carbohydrate; 2mg Cholesterol; 249mg Sodium*

Savory Pull-Apart

Preparing this while the dough is still frozen couldn't be easier!
Assemble this bread a day ahead and bake it the next.

1/4 cup grated Parmesan cheese
3 tablespoons sesame seeds
1/2 teaspoon crushed dried basil
1 27-ounce package (18 rolls) frozen rolls
1/4 cup butter, melted

Make Ahead

Thoroughly grease a 10" fluted tube pan.

In a small bowl, combine Parmesan cheese, sesame seeds, and basil. Add about one-third of the mixture to greased pan; lift and turn pan to coat the sides and bottom. Place 9 of the frozen rolls in the pan; drizzle with half the butter. Sprinkle half of the remaining cheese mixture on top. Add remaining rolls. Drizzle with remaining butter and sprinkle with remaining cheese mixture. Cover; let rolls thaw and rise overnight (12 to 24 hours) in refrigerator. The next day let stand at room temperature for 30 minutes. Bake at 350°F for 20 minutes. Cover and bake 15 minutes more or until golden. Remove bread from pan onto a wire rack. Serve warm.

Makes 8 servings. Per serving: *353 Calories; 13g Fat; 11g Protein; 50g Carbohydrate; 17mg Cholesterol, 601mg Sodium*

Tarragon Rolls

Arabs brought tarragon to France from the plains of Siberia in the fifteenth century.*
It adds a delicate and unique flavor to these light rolls.

Make Ahead

- 2 1/2 cups all-purpose flour, divided
- 1 package active dry yeast
- 1 tablespoon dried parsley
- 2 teaspoons crushed dried tarragon
- 1 teaspoon celery seed
- 1 cup warm (115° to 120°F) water
- 2 tablespoons sugar
- 2 tablespoons vegetable oil
- 1/2 teaspoon salt
- 1 egg or 1/4 cup Morningstar Farms® *Scramblers®*

In a large mixer bowl, combine 1 1/2 cups of the flour, yeast, parsley, tarragon, and celery seed.

In a separate bowl, stir together the water, sugar, oil, and salt. Add to the flour mixture; add egg. Beat at low speed of electric mixer for 1/2 minute, scraping bowl. Beat 3 minutes at high speed. Using dough hook or spoon, stir in the remaining flour, adding extra if needed until dough is no longer sticky. Place in a greased bowl and grease the top of the dough. Cover; let rise until double (about 30 minutes). Spoon into 12 greased muffin cups, filling each slightly more than half full. Cover; let rise until nearly double (20 to 30 minutes). Bake at 375°F for 15 to 18 minutes.

Makes 12 servings. Per serving: *134 Calories; 3g Fat; 4g Protein; 23g Carbohydrate; 18mg Cholesterol; 97mg Sodium*

Ambrosia

BY PATRICIA ROSE

Ambrosia was the food of the gods and goddesses of Greek mythology. Debi fondly recalls having this "heavenly" salad for special occasions and holiday meals. It was a tradition in her childhood home.

- 2 cups cubed cantaloupe
- 1 20-ounce can pineapple chunks in juice, drained, halved
- 1/4 cup rinsed, halved maraschino cherries
- 2 cups stemmed, quartered strawberries
- 1 11-ounce can mandarin oranges in light syrup, drained
- 4 cups miniature marshmallows
- 1 cup coconut flakes
- 1 cup light sour cream
- 1 cup whipping cream
- 3 tablespoons powdered sugar
- 1 teaspoon vanilla
- 1 banana, sliced

Mix together fruits (except banana), marshmallows, coconut, and sour cream. Refrigerate overnight. Just before serving, whip the cream, adding powdered sugar and vanilla, beating until stiff. Fold whipped cream and banana into fruit.

Note: *Any combination of fruit can be used. The great thing about this salad is that more fruit and/or marshmallows can be added to make it "stretch" if needed!*

Makes 12 servings. Per serving: *223 Calories; 10g Fat; 2g Protein; 33g Carbohydrate; 29mg Cholesterol; 45mg Sodium*

B. C. P. Salad

Mark Twain once said, "Cauliflower is nothing but a cabbage with a college education."* This salad, using cauliflower and other good things, has a nice mix of crunchy and smooth textures.

Make Ahead

- 4 cups small broccoli florets
- 4 cups small cauliflower florets
- 1 20-ounce package frozen petite peas, unthawed
- 1 8-ounce can sliced water chestnuts, chopped
- 3 scallions or green onions, finely sliced
- 1 1-ounce package ranch salad dressing mix
- 1 cup light mayonnaise
- 1 cup light sour cream
- 1 cup halved cherry tomatoes (for garnish)

In a large bowl, mix broccoli, cauliflower, frozen peas, water chestnuts, and onion.

In a small bowl, whisk the dressing mix, mayonnaise, and sour cream, blending thoroughly; add to vegetables. After mixing, refrigerate the salad at least 3 hours (overnight is better). Garnish with cherry tomatoes before serving.

Makes 12 servings. Per serving: *96 Calories; 2g Fat; 5g Protein; 16g Carbohydrate; 10mg Cholesterol; 352mg Sodium*

Danish Red Cabbage

BY RICHARD ROSE

The Danish heritage of Debi's dad comes through each time he makes this special dish for family get-togethers. Since cabbage is 91 percent water, not much added liquid is required.

- 1 head red cabbage (3 pounds)
- 2 tablespoons vinegar
- 1/4 cup butter
- 1/3 cup sugar
- 1 teaspoon salt
- 2/3 cup red currant jelly
- 1 apple, cored and cubed

Wash and quarter cabbage. Remove inner stalk. Finely chop the cabbage and sprinkle with vinegar so that it does not turn black.

Melt butter in a 4 1/2-quart pot; add sugar and salt. Add cabbage and cook slowly for 15 minutes. Add the rest of the ingredients and simmer about 2 hours. Reheat at serving time, if needed.

Makes 8 servings. Per serving: *190 Calories; 6g Fat; 2g Protein; 35g Carbohydrate; 15mg Cholesterol; 337mg Sodium*

Mango Salad

Did you know that more fresh mangos are eaten every day than any other fruit in the world?* As Debi was growing up, her mother often made this mango salad. The recipe was rediscovered as Debi went through her mother's recipe box.

Make Ahead

2 cups boiling water
1 6-ounce package lemon gelatin
1 teaspoon lemon juice
1/8 teaspoon salt
1 28-ounce can mangos in syrup, undrained
1 8-ounce package fat-free cream cheese, softened

Dissolve gelatin in boiling water. Stir in lemon juice and salt.

Purée mango with syrup and cream cheese in blender or food processor until smooth; add to gelatin. Pour mixture in serving bowl and refrigerate, covered, until set.

Makes 12 servings. Per serving: *133 Calories; 0g Fat; 4g Protein; 25g Carbohydrate; 3mg Cholesterol; 170mg Sodium*

Apple Dumpling Slices

The saying goes, "As American as apple pie." The United States may specialize in apple pastries, but China actually grows more apples than the U.S.A.!* Just consider this tasty apple creation as a form of America's favorite dessert.

- 1 cup sugar
- 1 1/2 cups water
- 1 1/2 cups flour
- 2 teaspoons baking powder
- 1/2 teaspoon salt
- 1/2 cup vegetable shortening
- 1/3 cup 2% milk, room temperature
- 1 teaspoon cinnamon
- 2 apples, peeled, chopped fine
- 1/2 cup chopped pecans
- 1/2 cup butter

In a medium saucepan over medium heat, stir sugar and water until sugar melts.

In a mixing bowl, mix flour, baking powder, and salt. Cut shortening into flour using a pastry blender or fork. Add milk, stir with fork only until dough leaves sides of bowl. Turn out onto lightly floured surface and knead until smooth. Roll out into a 10" x 14" rectangle.

Mix cinnamon with apples and pecans. Spread evenly over dough. Roll up dough from long side, jelly-roll style. Dampen edge of dough and seal. Slice dough into 15 slices.

Melt butter in a 9" x 13" baking dish at 350°F. Place dough slices, cut side down, in pan with melted butter. Pour sugar-water over and around rolls. (It will look like too much liquid, but the crust will absorb it.) Bake at 350°F for 45 to 50 minutes until golden.

Makes 15 servings. Per serving: *250 Calories; 16g Fat; 2g Protein; 27g Carbohydrate; 21mg Cholesterol; 185mg Sodium*

Blueberry Macaroon Torte

Bluberries and coconut macaroons are two of Debi's absolute favorite things. This dessert combines the two into one. The alternate version is for our friend Tony.

Make Ahead

- 4 egg whites or 1 cup Egg Beaters® Egg Whites
- 3/4 cup sugar
- 1 tablespoon lemon juice
- 2 teaspoons vanilla, divided
- 1/2 teaspoon almond extract
- 3 tablespoons flour
- 1/2 teaspoon baking powder
- 1 cup finely ground blanched almonds
- 1 1/4 cups sweetened coconut flakes
- 2/3 cup blueberry preserves
- 2 1/2 cups fresh or frozen blueberries (if using frozen, thaw and drain)
- 1/2 cup whipping cream
- 3 tablespoons powdered sugar

Beat egg whites until foamy; gradually beat in sugar until soft peaks form. Add lemon juice, 1 teaspoon vanilla, and almond extract. Continue beating at high speed until whites form stiff, shiny peaks.

Combine flour, baking powder, almonds, and coconut; then fold into beaten whites until very well mixed. *Do not overbeat.* Turn mixture into a greased and floured 9" springform pan, spreading it so that the sides are much higher than the center. Bake at 325°F for 35 to 40 minutes or until top is firm and lightly browned and sides shrink away from pan. Cool completely in pan on a wire rack; remove from pan and place on a serving platter.

For filling, heat preserves in a small saucepan just until melted. Stir in blueberries and completely coat with sauce. Spread blueberry mixture over top of macaroon base. Chill until shortly before serving time.

Whip the cream, adding powdered sugar and 1 teaspoon vanilla, beating until stiff. Use a pastry bag to decorate berry filling with a circle of whipped cream stars (or just make small dollops).

Makes 8 servings. Per serving: *406 Calories; 19g Fat; 7g Protein; 57g Carbohydrate; 20mg Cholesterol; 101mg Sodium*

PIÑA COLADA TORTE *(alternative)*

In meringue, omit lemon juice. Replace almond extract with coconut extract. In place of almonds, use macadamia nuts.

For filling, replace the blueberry perserves and blueberries with the following:

- 1 20-ounce can crushed pineapple, with juice
- 1/2 cup water
- 1/2 cup sugar
- 3 tablespoons cornstarch
- 1/3 cup cold water
- 1/2 teaspoon pineapple extract

In a medium saucepan, heat pineapple, 1/2 cup water, and sugar to boiling. Mix cornstarch and 1/3 cup cold water in a small cup and pour slowly into the pineapple, stirring constantly. Cook until thick. Remove from heat, stir in extract, and let cool 1 hour.

To assemble, leave the macaroon base in the pan. Pour the cooled pineapple over base and chill in the pan. To serve, remove from pan and decorate with whipped cream as directed.

Cherry Brown Betty

The "Betty," which is a baked pudding made with fruit and bread crumbs, dates back to colonial America. Often made with apples, this Betty is made with cherries because our daughter Stacey's favorite fruit is cherries. This dessert is both special for her and a tribute to her 100+-year-old great-grandmother, Bertha Parmentier. You see, we found the recipe in "Mom-Mom's" things, written in her own hand on the back of an envelope dated 1953.

2 14.5-ounce cans pie cherries
3 cups fresh bread crumbs
1/4 cup butter, melted
1/2 cup sugar
3/4 teaspoon cinnamon
Dash salt
1 teaspoon grated lemon peel
2 teaspoons lemon juice

Drain cherries, reserving 1/2 cup of juice.

Place bread crumbs in a medium bowl. Gradually drizzle butter over crumbs, stirring constantly. Add sugar, cinnamon, salt, and lemon peel. Mix well. Add cherries and stir. Transfer mixture into a greased 7" x 11" baking dish.

Mix reserved cherry juice and lemon juice and pour over cherry-crumb mixture. Bake at 400°F for 20 to 25 minutes or until lightly browned on top. Serve warm with whipped cream or ice cream if desired.

Makes 8 servings. Per serving: *166 Calories; 6g Fat; 2g Protein; 27g Carbohydrate; 15mg Cholesterol; 106mg Sodium*

Chess Pie

BY JEANNE PEDERSEN

In colonial America, Chess Pie was a simple filling of eggs, butter, sugar, and lemon.*
This version has walnuts and coconut with a lattice-crust topping.
It was a favorite dessert of Jim's dad.

2/3 cup vegetable shortening
2 cups all-purpose flour
1 teaspoon salt
4 tablespoons cold water
1/2 cup butter
1 cup sugar
3 eggs or 3/4 cup Morningstar Farms® *Scramblers®*
1 cup chopped walnuts
1 cup sweetened coconut flakes
1 teaspoon vanilla
Pinch salt

Make Ahead

Cut shortening into flour and salt until particles are size of small peas. Sprinkle in water, 1 tablespoon at a time, tossing with fork until all flour is moistened and pastry pulls together into a ball (1 to 2 additional teaspoons water can be added if necessary). Divide pastry into halves and shape into two rounds. Roll pastry 2 inches larger than inverted pie plate. Place one pastry circle in pie plate; trim to 1/2" from rim.

Cream together butter and sugar. Add eggs, nuts, coconut, vanilla, and salt. Pour into unbaked pie shell.

Roll out second pastry as before. Cut into strips and form into a lattice pattern across the top. Fold bottom crust over edges and flute. Bake at 350°F for 30 to 40 minutes.

Makes 8 servings. Per serving: *633 Calories; 43g Fat; 10g Protein; 55g Carbohydrate; 120mg Cholesterol; 432mg Sodium*

Chocolate Cheese Pie

It is said that Napoleon carried chocolate with him on his military campaigns and always ate it when he needed quick energy. This frozen chocolate dessert is our daughter Lisa's favorite pie. It's really rich, so one pie will serve a lot of people.

Make Ahead

- 1 1/2 cups (about 20 squares) graham cracker crumbs
- 3/4 cup + 3 tablespoons sugar, divided
- 1/3 cup margarine, melted
- 1 cup or 1 6-ounce package semisweet chocolate chips
- 1 8-ounce package fat-free cream cheese, softened
- 1 teaspoon vanilla
- 1/4 teaspoon salt
- 1 cup heavy cream, whipped

Make crust by combining graham cracker crumbs and 3 tablespoons sugar; add margarine and mix thoroughly. Press into 9" pie plate. Bake at 350°F for 10 minutes; cool.

For filling, place chocolate chips in a small bowl and microwave just long enough so they finish melting when stirred, about 1 to 1 1/2 minutes. Let cool.

With an electric mixer in a medium bowl, blend cream cheese, 3/4 cup sugar, vanilla, and salt. Add melted chocolate, beating until smooth. Fold in whipped cream until blended completely. Pour filling into shell. Cover and freeze. Remove from freezer 5 to 10 minutes before serving.

Makes 12 servings. Per serving: *300 Calories; 17g Fat; 4g Protein; 36g Carbohydrate; 30mg Cholesterol; 256mg Sodium*

Créme Brûlée

This is an extravagant but very classy dessert. We've cut down on some of the richness and calories. However, if you want to "go for the gold," use all heavy cream.

2 cups heavy cream
2 cups half-and-half
1/2 cup + approximately 3 tablespoons sugar
1/8 teaspoon salt
6 egg yolks
2 teaspoons vanilla extract

Make Ahead

Prepare a pot of boiling water.

In a saucepan over medium heat, combine cream, half-and-half, 1/2 cup sugar, and salt; cook, stirring occasionally, until steam rises, 4 to 5 minutes.

In a bowl, beat egg yolks and vanilla until smooth. Pour hot cream into yolks, a little at a time, stirring constantly, until blended. Strain mixture through a fine mesh sieve set over a bowl. Skim off bubbles. Slowly divide mixture among eight 3-ounce ramekins.

Line the bottom of a 10" x 15" baking dish (or two 8" x 8") with a paper or cloth kitchen towel. Place ramekins in the baking dish(es) and add boiling water to fill pan(s) halfway up sides of ramekins. Bake at 300°F until custard is just set, 40 to 50 minutes. Remove from the oven and leave in the water bath until cool. Take from water bath and chill for 2 hours or up to 2 days. To serve, sprinkle approximately 1 teaspoon sugar evenly over each custard. Set broiler to the highest setting and place ramekins on a baking sheet. Position the ramekins no more than 5 inches away from the heat source. Broil for 2 to 3 minutes, until the sugar is melted, bubbly, and browned. (Or, use a small kitchen torch, following the instructions, and serve without further refrigeration.) Rechill custards a few minutes before serving.

Note: *Custard cups can be used in place of ramekins.*

Makes 8 servings. Per serving: *378 Calories; 33g Fat; 5g Protein; 17g Carbohydrate; 263mg Cholesterol; 86mg Sodium*

Dulce de Leche Cheesecake

Our friend, Tony Anobile, introduced us to the taste of dulce de leche. Jim created this cheesecake in Tony's honor. It has a wonderful caramel-cream flavor that is hard to resist!

- 1 14-ounce can fat-free sweetened condensed milk
- 1 cup graham cracker crumbs
- 1/4 cup brown sugar
- 1/4 cup (plus additional) butter, melted
- 3 8-ounce packages fat-free cream cheese, softened
- 3/4 cup sugar
- 2 1/2 teaspoons cornstarch
- 2 eggs or 1/2 cup Morningstar Farms® *Scramblers®*
- 1 teaspoon vanilla
- 1/2 cup whipping cream

To make the dulce de leche, remove the label from the can of sweetened condensed milk. Place the unopened can in a large pan and cover completely with water. Bring to a boil, reduce heat to a slow boil, and continue boiling for 2 hours 20 minutes (make sure that water covers the can at all times). Remove from water and cool for at least 30 minutes.

For crust, combine the graham cracker crumbs and brown sugar; add the melted butter. Use additional butter to grease the sides only of a 9" springform pan. Sprinkle to coat the sides with a small amount of crumb mixture. Press remaining crumbs into the bottom of the pan. Place in the refrigerator or freezer for 30 minutes.

For the filling, whip the cream cheese in a mixer. With the mixer running slowly, sprinkle in the sugar and cornstarch; then add in the eggs, one at a time, and the vanilla. Slowly add the cream until all ingredients are well mixed. Pour half the filling into a medium bowl. Add half the can of dulce de leche into the bowl of filling; mix well. Pour into the springform pan. Pour the remaining filling over the first layer. With a knife, gently swirl the two layers. Drizzle the remaining dulce de leche over the top and again swirl with a knife, if desired. Bake at 350°F for 50 to 60 minutes (or until the top begins to brown and the cake is firm). Cool at room temperature. Run knife between cake and pan sides. Refrigerate overnight.

Makes 12 servings. Per serving: *334 Calories; 9g Fat; 12g Protein; 50g Carbohydrate; 73mg Cholesterol; 400mg Sodium*

Greek Lemon Rice

BY PATRICIA ROSE

The Greek influence is felt here with the simple combination of lemon and rice in a sweet pudding-type dessert. Debi's grandmother passed this recipe to her daughter, who made it for Debi when she was a child. It brings a taste of "home" when we make it now.

- 2 cups water
- 1 scant teaspoon salt
- 1 cup white rice
- 2/3 cup sugar
- 2/3 cup 2% milk
- 1/3 cup low-fat evaporated milk
- 1 egg, beaten, or 1/4 cup Morningstar Farms® *Scramblers®*
- 1 teaspoon lemon extract
- 2 tablespoons lemon peel

In a medium saucepan, bring water and salt to a boil. Add rice and stir with a fork. Return to a boil, cover, and turn to lowest heat. Cook until water is absorbed. Let cool in the pan, stirring to fluff.

Meanwhile, in a small bowl mix the sugar, milk, evaporated milk, and egg. Add to the cooked rice. Cook over low heat until thickened, stirring constantly. Remove from heat and add lemon extract and peel. Chill.

Makes 8 servings. Per serving: *176 Calories; 1g Fat; 4g Protein; 37g Carbohydrate; 30mg Cholesterol; 298mg Sodium*

Loma Linda Chocolate Prune Cake

Growing up in Loma Linda, Debi enjoyed this cake as often as possible.
Don't let the name fool you! It's a moist, flavorful cake that even kids will like.

1/4 cup boiling water
25 (3/4 cup) pitted prunes
2/3 cup oil
1 cup sugar
1/2 cup + 2 tablespoons cocoa powder
2 teaspoons cinnamon
1 1/4 teaspoons salt, divided
1 1/2 teaspoons vanilla, divided
2 eggs or 1/2 cup Morningstar Farms® *Scramblers*®
1 cup buttermilk
2 1/2 cups flour
1 1/2 teaspoons baking soda
2 teaspoons baking powder
1/4 cup water
1/4 cup vegetable shortening
1/4 cup light corn syrup
5 cups powdered sugar, sifted

Soak prunes 30 minutes in boiling water.

In bowl of electric mixer, combine oil, sugar, 2 tablespoons cocoa, cinnamon, 1 teaspoon salt, and 1 teaspoon vanilla. Add eggs one at a time, beating for 1 minute after each addition.

Combine prunes (including unabsorbed water) and buttermilk in blender and purée.

Sift together flour, soda, and baking powder. Alternatly add flour and buttermilk to creamed mixture, beginning and ending with flour. Beat about 15 seconds. Pour into 2 greased and floured 8" or 9" cake pans. Bake at 350°F for 30 minutes. Cool 10 minutes in pans. Loosen sides and invert onto greased racks to cool completely.

FROSTING: Bring water to a boil; transfer to mixer bowl. Beat in shortening and corn syrup. Add powdered sugar, 1/2 cup cocoa, 1/4 teaspoon salt, and 1/2 teaspoon vanilla. Cream well to spreading consistency. Fill and frost cooled cake.

Makes 16 servings. Per serving: *445 Calories; 14g Fat; 4g Protein; 80g Carbohydrate; 29mg Cholesterol; 362mg Sodium*

Pineapple Upside-Down Cake

BY PATRICIA ROSE

This cake is best made in a cast-iron skillet. But if you don't have one, by all means make it anyway in a regular cake pan. Debi's dad has always had a special liking for this dessert.

3 tablespoons butter
1 20-ounce can pineapple slices in juice, drained—reserve juice
2/3 cup brown sugar
7 maraschino cherries
12 pecan halves
1/3 cup vegetable shortening
1/2 cup granulated sugar
1 egg or 1/4 cup Morningstar Farms® *Scramblers®*
1 teaspoon vanilla
1 1/2 cups cake flour, sifted
1 1/2 teaspoons baking powder
1/2 teaspoon salt

TOPPING: Melt butter in 9" or 10" cast-iron skillet (or greased similar-size cake pan). Drain pineapple, reserving 3/4 cup liquid. Sprinkle brown sugar over bottom of pan. Arrange 7 pineapple slices over sugar and place 1 maraschino cherry in center of each ring. Arrange pecan halves in each space between pineapple.

CAKE: Cream together shortening and granulated sugar; add egg and vanilla; beat until fluffy. Sift together dry ingredients; add alternately with reserved pineapple juice, beginning and ending with flour, beating well after each addition. Spread gently over pineapple so as to not disturb arrangement of the fruit. Bake at 350°F for 45 to 50 minutes or until cake tester comes out clean and cake is golden. Let stand 5 minutes; invert on plate. Serve warm with whipped cream if desired.

Makes 8 servings. Per serving: *357 Calories; 16g Fat; 3g Protein; 52g Carbohydrate; 43mg Cholesterol; 266mg Sodium*

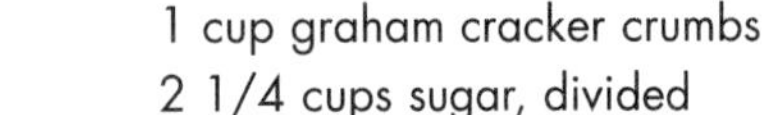

Jim began developing his cheesecake expertise for church-office Christmas parties held at the Pedersen home. Now these desserts appear around the conference office. This one is a favorite of several of the secretaries.

- 1 cup graham cracker crumbs
- 2 1/4 cups sugar, divided
- 1 1/4 cups finely chopped coconut flakes, divided
- 1/4 cup (plus additional) butter, melted
- 3 8-ounce packages fat-free cream cheese, softened
- 3 tablespoons cornstarch, divided
- 2 eggs or 1/2 cup Morningstar Farms® *Scramblers®*
- 1 teaspoon coconut extract
- 1/2 cup coconut milk
- 1 20-ounce can crushed pineapple in juice, undrained
- 2 teaspoons lemon juice
- 3 tablespoons cold water

CRUST: Combine the graham cracker crumbs, 1/2 cup sugar, and 1/4 cup coconut; add 1/4 cup melted butter. Use additional butter to grease the sides only of a 9" springform pan; sprinkle to coat the sides with a small amount of crumb mixture. Press remaining crumbs into the bottom of the pan. Place in the refrigerator or freezer for 30 minutes.

FILLING: Whip the cream cheese in a mixer. With the mixer running slowly, sprinkle in 1 cup sugar and 1 tablespoon cornstarch; then add the eggs one at a time followed by the coconut extract. Slowly add the coconut milk. Add 1/2 cup coconut and mix just until all ingredients are well blended. Pour into the prepared pan. Bake at 350°F for 40 to 45 minutes (or until the top begins to brown and the cake is firm). Cool at room temperature.

TOPPING: Mix together the pineapple, 3/4 cup sugar, and lemon juice in a medium saucepan. Bring to a medium boil. In small bowl or cup stir together 2 tablespoons cornstarch and water and pour into the boiling pineapple mixture, stirring constantly until thickened. Allow to cool for at least 30 minutes. Pour over warm cheesecake. Cool to room temperature. Run a knife between cake and pan sides. Refrigerate overnight.

In a small skillet, toast 1/2 cup coconut over low heat until golden, stirring often. Garnish cheesecake with toasted coconut flakes.

Makes 12 servings. Per serving: *385 Calories; 10g Fat; 10g Protein; 63g Carbohydrate; 55mg Cholesterol; 387mg Sodium*

Pumpkin Cheesecake

Did you know that championship pumpkins weigh in at over 800 pounds? Pumpkins can grow 10 to 15 pounds per day!* You don't need that large a pumpkin in order to make this recipe. It is especially good around holiday times, but feel free to make it any time of the year.

- 1 cup graham cracker crumbs
- 1/3 cup finely chopped pecans
- 1 1/2 cups + 3 tablespoons sugar, divided
- 1 3/4 teaspoons pumpkin pie spice, divided
- 6 tablespoons butter, melted
- 3 8-ounce packages fat-free cream cheese, softened
- 1 tablespoon cornstarch
- 3 eggs or 3/4 cup Morningstar Farms® *Scramblers®*
- 3/4 cup whipping cream
- 1 15-ounce can pumpkin
- 4 teaspoons vanilla, divided
- 1 pint light sour cream

CRUST: Mix graham cracker crumbs, nuts, 3 tablespoons sugar, and 1/4 teaspoon pumpkin pie spice. Stir in butter. Press mixture evenly on bottom of 10" springform pan. Bake at 350°F for 10 minutes. Cool. Reduce oven temperature to 325°F.

FILLING: Blend cream cheese with 1 cup sugar and cornstarch until smooth. Add eggs one at a time, beating until blended. Add whipping cream, pumpkin, 2 teaspoons vanilla, and 1 1/2 teaspoons pumpkin pie spice, blending thoroughly. Pour into crust. Bake at 325°F for 90 minutes or until set, checking regularly after 60 minutes. Remove and let rest 10 minutes.

TOPPING: Blend sour cream, 1/2 cup sugar, and 2 teaspoons vanilla until smooth. Pour topping over cheesecake. Cool to room temperature. Run knife between cake and pan sides. Chill cake uncovered overnight.

Note: *As an option, add 1/2 teaspoon cinnamon to the sour cream topping and drizzle caramel syrup over each slice of cheesecake just prior to serving.*

Makes 12 servings. Per serving: *379 Calories; 16g Fat; 12g Protein; 47g Carbohydrate; 102mg Cholesterol; 403mg Sodium*

Raspberry Sour-Cream Pie

The "berry battle" is alive and well in our house! Which berry is the most popular? National statistics indicate that our daughters' favorite strawberries are #1 in popularity, Debi's blueberries are #2, and Jim's raspberries come in #3.* But one taste of this pie just might convert you to Jim's viewpoint!

1 1/3 cups all-purpose flour, divided
1/3 cup vegetable shortening
1/2 teaspoon salt
3 tablespoons cold water
3/4 cup + 2 tablespoons sugar, divided
2 cups light sour cream
1/2 teaspoon clear vanilla
3 cups fresh raspberries
1/4 cup fresh bread crumbs
2 tablespoons butter, melted

Cut shortening into 1 cup flour and salt until particles are size of small peas. Sprinkle in water, 1 tablespoon at a time, tossing with fork until all flour is moistened and pastry pulls together into a ball (1 to 2 additional teaspoons water can be added if necessary). Shape into a round. Roll pastry 2 inches larger than inverted pie plate. Place pastry circle in pie plate; trim to 1/2" from rim. Fold crust up and crimp edges.

In a bowl, combine 3/4 cup sugar and 1/3 cup flour. Whisk in the sour cream and vanilla. Arrange raspberries evenly in the pie shell. Spread sour cream mixture over berries.

Combine bread crumbs, 2 tablespoons sugar, and melted butter. Sprinkle over pie. Bake at 400°F for 30 to 40 minutes or until pastry and filling are golden. Cool on rack. Serve same day at room temperature.

Makes 8 servings. Per serving: *307 Calories; 13g Fat; 4g Protein; 45g Carbohydrate; 17mg Cholesterol; 181mg Sodium*

Strawberry Shortcake Trifle

Did you know that strawberries are the only fruit with the seeds on the outside?
Lisa, our youngest, loves strawberries. This trifle is in her honor.
It's not too sweet and is a great light summer dessert.

- 1 quart fresh strawberries
- 2 tablespoons sugar
- 2 cups prepared vanilla pudding
- 1 3-ounce package cream cheese, softened
- 2 4.5-ounce package dessert cups or pound cake may be substitued

Make-Ahead

Reserve 1 to 3 berries, depending on size, for garnish. Hull and slice 1/2 of the remaining berries. Arrange 1/2 of the sliced berries on bottom and along sides of a clear medium-sized trifle dish or bowl.

Hull and place remaining unsliced berries in blender or food processor; add sugar. Blend until puréed.

In a mixer bowl, beat pudding and cream cheese with an electric mixer on medium speed until smooth.

Place 1/2 of the cake in the bottom of the dish. Pour 1/2 of the puréed berries over cake, then 1/2 of the pudding mixture and the remaining sliced berries. Repeat layers with remaining cake, puréed berries, and pudding. Garnish with reserved whole berries.

Makes 8 servings. Per serving: *255 Calories; 9g Fat; 4g Protein; 42g Carbohydrate; 30mg Cholesterol; 315mg Sodium*

Chapter 5: Make-at-the-Last-Minute Dishes

Crusty Parmesan Biscuits

Did you know that Parmesan cheese quite possibly originated in Parma, Italy, in the eleventh century?* When you don't have the time or energy to roll out biscuits, this drop version fits the bill for that extra addition to your meal.

- 1 3/4 cups flour
- 1 tablespoon baking powder
- 1/2 teaspoon salt
- 1/4 cup grated Parmesan cheese
- 1/2 cup butter
- 1/2 cup 2% milk
- 1 egg, slightly beaten, or 1/4 cup Morningstar Farms® *Scramblers®*

Combine dry ingredients and cheese. Cut in butter until mixture resembles coarse crumbs.

Combine milk and egg; add to dry ingredients just until moistened. Spoon 1/4 cup of dough for each biscuit onto a cookie sheet. Bake at 400°F for 12 to 15 minutes or until golden.

Makes 10 servings. Per serving: *183 Calories; 11g Fat; 4g Protein; 18g Carbohydrate; 48mg Cholesterol; 358mg Sodium*

Herb Flatbread

A quick version of restaurant focaccia, this bread starts with a ready-made pizza crust but tastes completely "homemade."

Last Min.

- 1 10-ounce package refrigerated pizza crust
- 1 1/2 tablespoons olive oil, divided
- 1/2 teaspoon dried thyme
- 1/2 teaspoon dried marjoram
- 1/2 teaspoon dried rosemary
- 1/2 teaspoon dried basil
- 1/4 cup (about 6) oil-packed sun-dried tomatoes, drained and chopped
- 1/3 cup softened goat cheese
- 2 eggs, room temperature, or 1/2 cup Morningstar Farms® *Scramblers®*

Spread dough evenly over bottom of a greased 9" x 13" baking dish. With your fingers, make indentations all over the surface of the dough. Brush with 1 tablespoon olive oil. Mix herbs. Sprinkle dough with tomatoes and half of the herbs.

In a medium bowl, combine cheese, eggs, remaining oil, and remaining herbs. Whisk together well. Pour evenly over tomatoes. Bake at 400°F for 15 to 20 minutes, until edges are golden brown.

Makes 12 servings. Per serving: *109 Calories; 5g Fat; 4g Protein; 12g Carbohydrate; 39mg Cholesterol; 198mg Sodium*

Salsa Muffins

These muffins make a nice accompaniment to Mexican meals and are a good way to use up that extra salsa from the fridge. There are many different salsa blends on the market, so be creative in what you choose to use. Each one will produce a unique and special flavor.

1 cup salsa
1/3 cup vegetable oil
1/4 cup 2% milk
1 egg or 1/4 cup Morningstar Farms® *Scramblers®*
2 cups all-purpose flour
2 teaspoons baking powder
1/2 teaspoon baking soda
1/4 teaspoon salt

In a medium bowl, beat the salsa, oil, milk, and egg. Stir in remaining ingredients just until flour is moistened (batter will be lumpy). Spoon batter into 12 muffin cups with only the bottoms greased. Bake at 375°F for 20 to 25 minutes or until golden brown. Immediately remove from pan.

Makes 12 servings. Per serving: *147 Calories; 8g Fat; 3g Protein; 17g Carbohydrate; 18mg Cholesterol; 182mg Sodium*

Savory Pita Crisps

When you want something extra with your meal, but want something light, choose these pita crisps. They will disappear like magic.

- 3 large pita bread or 6 7-inch flour tortillas
- 1/4 cup butter or margarine, melted
- 1/4 cup snipped parsley
  or 1 tablespoon dried parsley flakes
- 1 teaspoon crushed dried oregano
- 1/8 teaspoon garlic powder
- 1/8 teaspoon onion powder
- 1/4 cup grated Parmesan
  or Romano cheese

Separate the pita bread into halves, forming 2 thin, round single layers from each pita bread.

In small mixing bowl, stir together the butter or margarine and seasonings. Brush a scant tablespoon of the mixture on the rough side of each pita half (or on 1 side of each tortilla). Sprinkle 2 teaspoons cheese on top of each circle. Cut each into 6 wedges. Arrange wedges in a single layer on ungreased baking sheets. Bake in a 350°F oven for 12 to 15 minutes or until crisp and golden brown. Serve warm or at room temperature. Makes 36 crisps.

Makes 8 servings. Per serving: *130 Calories; 7g Fat; 4g Protein; 14g Carbohydrate; 17mg Cholesterol; 233mg Sodium*

Toasted Garlic-Cheese Bread

Did you know that the average American eats almost 60 pounds of bread a year?*
Serving bread in this style just might increase your annual consumption!

- 2 tablespoons finely crushed bread crumbs
- 2 tablespoons grated Parmesan cheese
- 1 teaspoon dried parsley
- 1 teaspoon paprika
- 1/2 teaspoon garlic powder
- Dash salt
- 2 tablespoons butter, melted
- 2 tablespoons olive oil
- 6 French rolls, halved lengthwise (3 1/2 to 4 inches each)

Combine bread crumbs, cheese, and seasonings.

In another bowl combine butter and olive oil. Brush the cut side of each roll half with the butter mixture; then sprinkle with about 1 teaspoon seasoned crumbs. Place on baking sheet. Bake at 400°F for 10 minutes.

Makes 12 servings. Per serving: *95 Calories; 5g Fat; 2g Protein; 10g Carbohydrate; 6mg Cholesterol; 153mg Sodium*

Asparagus, Apple, and Chicken Salad

Did you know that in the warmth of spring, asparagus spears can grow several inches in a single day? Also true: The wonderful combination in this salad "tantalizes the tastebuds," according to one of our taster friends.

- 2 cups 1" pieces fresh asparagus
- 1/4 cup cider vinegar
- 1/4 cup vegetable oil
- 4 teaspoons honey
- 4 teaspoons chopped fresh parsley
- 1 teaspoon salt
- 1 13-ounce can Worthington® Meatless Chicken Diced, drained
- 1 red apple, diced
- 4 cups torn mixed greens

Cook asparagus in a small amount of water until crisp-tender, 3 to 4 minutes; drain and cool.

In a bowl, combine vinegar, oil, honey, parsley, and salt. Stir in the chicken, apple, and asparagus; toss. Serve over greens.

Makes 12 servings. Per serving: *81 Calories; 5g Fat; 4g Protein; 7g Carbohydrate; 0mg Cholesterol; 256mg Sodium*

Black Bean and Couscous Salad

Couscous is often considered to be a grain. In reality, it is tiny granules of pasta. The name comes from the Moroccan cooking pot in which it was prepared. In this salad, the couscous adds a complimentary texture to the black beans.

- 2 cups boiling water
- 2 cups couscous
- 3/4 cup olive oil
- 1/3 cup balsamic vinegar
- 3 cloves garlic, crushed
- 2 15-ounce cans black beans, rinsed and drained
- 1/2 teaspoon salt
- 1/2 cup crumbled feta cheese
- 2 fresh tomatoes, cut into wedges

Pour boiling water over couscous and let stand 5 minutes.

Combine olive oil and vinegar; add garlic.

Mix beans and couscous; add dressing and salt. Toss all together. Garnish with crumbled feta and tomatoes.

Makes 12 servings. Per serving: *294 Calories; 15g Fat; 8g Protein; 35g Carbohydrate; 4mg Cholesterol; 428mg Sodium*

Cabbage Salad With Pesto Dressing

Each summer in our garden we grow lots of sweet basil to use in making homemade pesto. We freeze it in bags, ready to pull out as needed. It's not just for pasta anymore!

1 small cabbage
3 carrots, peeled and grated
4 scallions, finely sliced,
  or 1 teaspoon onion powder
1 tablespoon chopped parsley
  or a mix of parsley, basil, and chervil
1/4 cup pine nuts, toasted
2/3 cup light mayonnaise
1/4 cup pesto
1/2 cup plain yogurt
Salt, to taste

Using a food processor or sharp knife, thinly slice the cabbage and place in a large bowl. Toss in the carrots, scallions, herbs, and half of the pine nuts.

Make dressing by stirring together the mayonnaise, pesto, and yogurt in a small bowl. Mix dressing into cabbage and add salt to taste. Sprinkle remaining pine nuts on top.

Makes 8 servings. Per serving: *134 Calories; 8g Fat; 5g Protein; 14g Carbohydrate; 13mg Cholesterol; 191mg Sodium*

California Bistro Salad

A popular restaurant in California serves a salad similar to this one.
We have attempted to duplicate the unique combination.

2 tablespoons butter
1/4 cup (packed) brown sugar
1 tablespoon dark corn syrup
1 1/2 cups pecan halves
1 head leaf lettuce, washed and dried
2 fresh pears (or apples), cored and diced
1 11-ounce can mandarin oranges
 in light syrup, drained
1/2 cup dried mixed fruit bits
1/2 cup golden raisin/dried cherry blend
3/4 cup diced Swiss cheese
 or crumbled feta cheese
2 avocados, diced
1/4 cup olive oil
2 tablespoons cider vinegar
2 tablespoons sugar
1 1/2 teaspoons poppy seeds
1 teaspoon chopped green onions
1/8 teaspoon paprika

To make candied nuts, line a cookie sheet with foil. Melt butter in a saucepan. Stir in the brown sugar and corn syrup. Cook and stir over medium heat for 2 minutes or until sugar dissolves. Cover pan; cook 1 minute more. Uncover; add pecans. Cook, stirring constantly, about 5 minutes or until nuts are slightly darker. Immediately pour mixture onto cookie sheet. Spread pecans onto a single layer. Cool. Break into pieces.

Chop the lettuce. Toss with fruit, cheese, avocados, and the candied nuts.

Make dressing by combining oil, vinegar, sugar, poppy seeds, onions, and paprika in blender or food processor. Just before serving, pour on only enough dressing to coat the salad and toss.

Makes 12 servings. Per serving: *335 Calories; 23g Fat; 5g Protein; 31g Carbohydrate; 12mg Cholesterol; 58mg Sodium*

Confetti Salad

BY SUZANNE ROSE

This salad was served to friends who don't really care for red cabbage. They liked it so well they had seconds and when offered the leftovers, jumped at the chance!

Last Min.

- 1/2 medium red cabbage, finely shredded
- 1 15-ounce can cannellini (white kidney) beans, drained and rinsed
- 1 11-ounce can mandarin oranges in light syrup, drained
- 2 large scallions, sliced (tops included)
- 3 tablespoons extra-virgin olive oil
- 2 tablespoons balsamic vinegar
- 2 tablespoons orange juice
- 1/2 teaspoon salt
- 3/4 cup walnut halves, toasted

In a large mixing bowl, combine cabbage, beans, oranges, and scallions.

Whisk together oil, vinegar, orange juice, and salt. Toss with cabbage until blended. Sprinkle walnuts over top.

Makes 12 servings. Per serving: *137 Calories; 8g Fat; 4g Protein; 13g Carbohydrate; 0mg Cholesterol; 177mg Sodium*

Fresh Mozzarella and Tomato Salad

Someone once said, "A world without tomatoes is like a string quartet without violins."*
Given the fact that there are more than 10,000 different varieties of tomatoes,
you shouldn't have difficulty finding one that will become a favorite.
Debi loves to grow the small yellow pear tomatoes and can't resist
throwing some on this salad when she makes it in the summer.

3/4 pound fresh mozzarella, sliced 1/4" thick
4 large red ripe tomatoes, sliced 1/4" thick
2 tablespoons basil chiffonade**
Salt, to taste
3 tablespoons olive oil or garlic olive oil

Last Min.

On a large serving platter, arrange rows or rings of alternating and slightly overlapping slices of mozzarella and tomatoes. Sprinkle the basil over them and add salt to taste. Drizzle a thin line of oil down the center of each row of slices, and serve.

Note: *Instead of mozzarella, crumbled feta cheese may be sprinkled over the tomatoes. The following may be added as desired: thinly sliced red onion, Kalamata olives, capers, chopped watercress or arugula, minced sun-dried tomatoes.*

*******Basil cut into thin strips.*

Makes 8 servings. Per serving: *163 Calories; 13g Fat; 10g Protein; 3g Carbohydrate; 15mg Cholesterol; 231mg Sodium*

Mediterranean Spinach Salad

Feta cheese, included in this salad, is a classic and famous Greek curd cheese whose tradition dates back thousands of years. It is still made by shepherds in the mountains of Greece. Originally made with goat's or sheep's milk, today feta is often made commercially with pasteurized cow's milk.* The combination of pine nuts, Kalamata olives, olive oil, lemon juice, and oregano, make this salad a real Mediterranean delight!

- 1/4 cup pine nuts
- 1 1/2 pounds fresh young spinach leaves, well washed and spun dry
- 1 sweet red onion, thinly sliced, or 1 1/2 teaspoons onion powder
- 1 cup Kalamata olives
- 1 cup crumbled feta cheese
- 1/4 cup olive oil
- 2 tablespoons fresh lemon juice
- 1 clove garlic, crushed
- 1 teaspoon fresh or 1/2 teaspoon dried oregano leaves
- 1/8 teaspoon salt
- 1/8 teaspoon sugar

Toast pine nuts by sautéing in a saucepan until golden.

Toss together the spinach, onion (if using onion powder, add to the dressing below), olives, and feta in a large bowl.

Whisk together the remaining ingredients. Drizzle just enough of the dressing over the salad to coat it; toss to combine. Sprinkle pine nuts over top.

Makes 6 servings. Per serving: *301 Calories; 23g Fat; 13g Protein; 16g Carbohydrate; 17mg Cholesterol; 1113mg Sodium*

Basmati and Nut Pilaf

Basmati is a small but long-grained aromatic rice with a nutlike flavor and aroma. The word *basmati* itself means "fragrant." This delicious rice has been cultivated in India and Pakistan for several thousand years.* The combination of ingredients in this recipe gives a decidedly Southeast Asian flavor.

- 1 1/4 cups basmati or long-grain white rice
- 2 tablespoons vegetable oil
- 1 small onion, finely chopped,
  or 1 tablespoon minced onion, rehydrated
- 1 clove garlic, crushed
- 1 large carrot, coarsely grated
- 1 teaspoon cumin seed
- 2 teaspoons ground coriander
- 1/8 teaspoon ground cardamom
- 2 cups vegetable broth or water
- 1 bay leaf
- 1/2 teaspoon salt
- 1/2 cup unsalted cashews
- 1/8 cup chopped fresh parsley or cilantro

Wash the rice in a sieve under running water. If there is time, soak the rice for 30 minutes; then drain well.

In a large shallow pan, gently fry the onion, garlic, and carrot in oil for 4 to 5 minutes. Stir in the rice and spices and cook 1 or 2 more minutes, so that the grains are coated in oil. Pour in the broth or water, add the bay leaf, and season with salt. Bring to a boil, cover, and simmer very gently for about 15 minutes. Remove from the heat without lifting the lid—this helps the rice to firm up and cook further. Leave for about 5 minutes. Discard the bay leaf. Stir in the nuts and check the seasoning. Transfer to a serving dish. Scatter the chopped parsley or cilantro over the mixture for garnish.

Makes 10 servings. Per serving: *159 Calories; 6g Fat; 3g Protein; 23g Carbohydrate; 0mg Cholesterol; 361mg Sodium*

Creamed Spinach

Many children seem to identify with the sentiments of the author of *How to Eat Like a Child*. Delia Ephron says, "On the subject of spinach: divide into little piles. Rearrange again into new piles. After five or six maneuvers, sit back and say you are full."* Fortunately, our children love this high-vitamin vegetable—especially the creamed version.

Last Min.

2 10-ounce packages frozen chopped spinach, thawed
4 tablespoons butter
1/4 medium onion, finely chopped, or 1 teaspoon onion powder
Pinch nutmeg
2 cloves garlic, crushed
1 1/2 tablespoons flour
1 cup half-and-half
1/2 teaspoon salt

Cook spinach according to package directions. Drain and press dry in a sieve.

Heat butter in a large saucepan. Add the onions, nutmeg, and garlic; sauté for 4 to 5 minutes or until onion is soft. Stir in the flour and half-and-half. Simmer for 2 minutes before adding the spinach. Mix well and season with salt.

Makes 6 servings. Per serving: *152 Calories; 13g Fat; 4g Protein; 8g Carbohydrate; 35mg Cholesterol; 364mg Sodium*

Green-Bean Bundles

These basic vegetables are known by a number of names: green beans, snap beans, string beans, to name a few. They can be flat or round. They don't even always have to be green. But, if you really want to have an impressive, delicious, and easy side dish, this is a great choice when fresh green beans are at their peak.

- 1 3/4 pounds fresh green beans
- 2 yellow squash, 1 1/2" diameter
- 1/4 cup olive oil
- 2 cloves garlic, minced
- 1/2 teaspoon dried tarragon

Rinse green beans. Snap off stem end.

Cut squash into 8 slices 3/4" thick; hollow out to 1/4-inch of rind. Place 10 to 12 beans into each squash ring. Steam the bundles by bringing a little water to a boil in a large saucepan; place bundles in a steamer basket and place basket in pan; steam, covered, just until tender, about 12 to 15 minutes.

Meanwhile, heat oil. Cook and stir garlic and tarragon in hot oil until garlic is soft but not brown. Place bundles on serving plate and pour garlic oil on top.

Makes 8 servings. Per serving: *106 Calories; 7g Fat; 3g Protein; 11g Carbohydrate; 0mg Cholesterol; 8mg Sodium*

Maple Glazed Carrots

Did you know that carrots were first grown as a medicine, not as a food? The name comes from the Greek word *karoto*. And "baby carrots" actually aren't baby at all, but are really a special variety cut into small shapes.

1 16-ounce package fresh baby carrots
1 tablespoon butter
1/4 cup maple syrup

Cook carrots in boiling salted water about 15 minutes, or just until tender; drain.

Simmer butter and syrup in a medium skillet for 2 minutes; add carrots. Cook over medium heat, turning often, about 8 minutes or until glazed.

Makes 6 servings. Per serving: *83 Calories; 2g Fat; 1g Protein; 15g Carbohydrate; 5mg Cholesterol; 45mg Sodium*

Quickest Corn in the West

BY CHARLA POOLEY

One day when our friend, Charla, was doing many things at once in the kitchen, she accidently dropped cream cheese in the corn she was making! The result is the easiest, creamiest, yummiest corn you'll ever eat!

- 2 16-ounce bags frozen petite white corn
- 1 8-ounce package fat-free cream cheese
- 1 tablespoon butter
- 1/2 teaspoon salt

Cook corn according to package directions. When almost cooked, add remaining ingredients and stir until smooth.

Makes 10 servings. Per serving: *118 Calories; 2g Fat; 6g Protein; 22g Carbohydrate; 7mg Cholesterol; 236mg Sodium*

Rice Pilaf

BY PATRICIA ROSE

Rice pilaf seems to have its origins in Turkish and Persian cuisine. The English mentioned pilaf as early as the seventeenth century, and the dish became popular after the British Empire spread through the Middle East and into India. The orzo pasta gives this easy pilaf an exotic touch. Debi's mother served it often.

- 1/4 cup butter
- 1 1/2 cups white rice
- 1/2 cup orzo pasta
- 1 envelope onion soup mix
- 4 cups very hot water
- 1/4 cup slivered almonds, toasted

Melt butter in a large skillet. Add rice and orzo; sauté until golden. Stir in onion soup mix and hot water. Bring to a boil, stir, then lower heat to the lowest simmer. Without removing lid, simmer until soft, about 20 to 25 minutes. Place in serving bowl and sprinkle with almonds.

Makes 8 servings. Per serving: *237 Calories; 9g Fat; 5g Protein; 35g Carbohydrate; 16mg Cholesterol; 501mg Sodium*

Spanish Rice

BY PATRICIA ROSE

When Debi's mother gave her this recipe and showed her how to make it, she used the terms *dash* and *pinch*—and for some things gave no measurements at all! She said, "Cook it until the consistency is just right," which Debi took note of as she watched. Cooking without exact measurements, and instead using the senses of sight, touch, and smell, is a sign of a great cook, which Debi's mother was. Through much trial and error, Debi has recreated her mother's version of Spanish Rice.

Last Min.

2 tablespoons oil
1/2 cup finely chopped onion
  or 1 tablespoon dehydrated onion
1/4 cup finely chopped green bell pepper
1 1/2 cups long-grain rice
1 14.5-ounce can Mexican-style stewed
  tomatoes, broken up
1 8-ounce can tomato sauce
2 1/2 cups hot water
1 teaspoon ground cumin
1/2 teaspoon salt
1 teaspoon oregano
1/2 teaspoon garlic powder
1/8 teaspoon sugar

Sauté onion and green pepper in oil until soft. Add rice and sauté until golden. Stir in remaining ingredients. Bring to a boil; lower heat to the lowest setting. Simmer, covered, for 30 minutes, stirring at 15 minutes to distribute ingredients. Stir again before serving.

Optional: *If desired, place in a greased 8" x 8" baking dish, cover with 1 cup grated cheddar cheese and 1 2.4-ounce can sliced olives (drained). Bake at 350°F for 10 minutes to melt the cheese.*

Makes 8 servings. Per serving: *153 Calories; 4g Fat; 1g Protein; 29g Carbohydrate; 0mg Cholesterol; 405mg Sodium*

Chicken Gravy

Helpful hint: When you boil potatoes (or other vegetables) and don't need the water for that meal, don't throw it away! Place it in plastic containers in usable amounts and freeze for a later date. If you're short on freezer space, zippered freezer bags that lie flat will work great too.

1/4 cup butter
1/4 cup flour
1 tablespoon chicken-style seasoning and broth mix
2 cups water from vegetables (potato water works well)

In a medium saucepan, melt butter over low heat. Blend in flour and chicken seasoning. Cook over low heat, stirring, until mixture is smooth and bubbly. Remove from heat. Stir in water. Bring to a boil, stirring constantly. Boil and stir 1 minute.

Makes 8 servings. Per serving: *68 Calories; 6g Fat; 0g Protein; 4g Carbohydrate; 15mg Cholesterol; 259mg Sodium*

Tomato Gravy

Browning the flour for this gravy gives it an earthy flavor, which makes it a great choice to serve with many of the entrees in this book. It's an old-fashioned technique that brings a real down-home taste.

- 1/4 cup flour
- 1/4 cup butter
- 1 tablespoon onion powder
- 2 cups tomato juice
- 1 teaspoon salt
- 1 teaspoon sugar

Brown flour in medium heavy skillet, stirring constantly until golden. Remove from skillet and set aside.

Melt butter in same skillet. Add flour and stir until blended. Cook over low heat about 2 minutes. Stir in remaining ingredients and continue cooking over low heat until thickened.

Variations: *In place of onion powder, sauté 1/2 cup chopped onion in the butter before adding flour. Or, add 2 tablespoons minced green bell pepper with the spices.*

Makes 8 servings. Per serving: *80 Calories; 6g Fat; 1g Protein; 7g Carbohydrate; 15mg Cholesterol; 545mg Sodium*

Vegex Gravy

Jim is the gravy maker of our family. It has become one of his specialties.
In fact, when Debi somehow ends up needing to make gravy, if he's not around,
she gets out his recipe!

Last Min.

- 3 cups water from vegetables (potato water works well)
- 1 tablespoon butter
- 1 tablespoon Vegex® yeast paste
- 1/4 teaspoon onion powder
- 1/4 teaspoon garlic powder
- 1 packet G. Washington's® Rich Brown Seasoning and Broth
- 1 teaspoon Kitchen Bouquet® liquid seasoning
- 3 tablespoons cornstarch
- 1/4 cup cold water

Put the vegetable water into a medium saucepan, begin heating. Add butter and seasonings. Taste and adjust seasoning to your taste. Bring to a slow boil.

Meanwhile, put the cornstarch into a cup or small bowl; add the cold water and stir until thoroughly mixed. Carefully add the cornstarch mixture to the boiling liquid, starting with about half, stirring the gravy constantly with a whisk. Add more cornstarch mixture until the gravy is at desired thickness.

Variations: *Add 1 cup sliced fresh mushrooms sautéed in 1 tablespoon butter. Or, for country-style gravy, use milk instead of vegetable water.*

Makes 12 servings. Per serving: *22 Calories; 7g Fat; 7g Protein; 3g Carbohydrate; 3mg Cholesterol; 163mg Sodium*

White Sauce

Some dishes, such as nut roasts or puff pastry creations, are enhanced by a wonderful sauce. The one we've included here can be dressed up or left alone, depending on the desired effect.

1/4 cup butter
1/4 cup flour
1/2 teaspoon salt
2 cups 2% milk

In a medium saucepan, melt butter over low heat. Blend in flour and salt. Cook over low heat, stirring, until mixture is smooth and bubbly. Remove from heat. Stir in milk. Bring to a boil, stirring constantly. Boil and stir 1 minute.

Variations: *For cheese sauce, remove sauce from heat, add 2 cups shredded cheddar or cubed processed American cheese to hot sauce and stir to melt. Or, add 2 tablespoons chopped fresh parsley (or 2 teaspoons dried) to sauce just before serving. Or, add 1/2 teaspoon onion powder with the flour.*

Makes 8 servings. Per serving: *95 Calories; 7g Fat; 2g Protein; 6g Carbohydrate; 20mg Cholesterol; 222mg Sodium*

Recipe Index

ENTREES

BAKED SIDE DISHES

SALADS AND NON-BAKED SIDE DISHES

BREADS

GRAVIES & SAUCES

DESSERTS

Product Index

$1.00 off — Manufacturer's Coupon — Expires 12/31/03 — $1.00 off

Save $1.00

on any ONE

product

Worthington Foods Inc.

CONSUMER: OFFER IS LIMITED TO ONE COUPON PER PACKAGE PURCHASED. COUPON MAY NOT BE REPRODUCED OR TRANSFERRED.
RETAILER: SPECIALTY FOODS INVESTMENT COMPANY will redeem this coupon in accordance with our redemption policy, copies available upon request. Cash value1/100¢. Void where prohibited, taxed, or restricted by law. Mail coupons to: KELLOGG COMPANY, P.O.BOX 870050, TECATE, CA 91987-0050.

41076

Redeemable at your local Adventist Book Center.
Not to be used in conjunction with any other offer.

Worthington and Morningstar Farms are trademarks of Specialty Foods Investment Company. TM, ® Specialty Foods Investment Company ©2002 Kellogg Company

5 28989 20076 6(8100)0 41076

$1.00 off — Manufacturer's Coupon — Expires 12/31/03 — $1.00 off

Save $1.00

on any ONE Natural Touch. product

from MORNINGSTAR Farms

Worthington Foods Inc.

CONSUMER: OFFER IS LIMITED TO ONE COUPON PER PACKAGE PURCHASED. COUPON MAY NOT BE REPRODUCED OR TRANSFERRED.
RETAILER: SPECIALTY FOODS INVESTMENT COMPANY will redeem this coupon in accordance with our redemption policy, copies available upon request. Cash value1/100¢. Void where prohibited, taxed, or restricted by law. Mail coupons to: SPECIALTY FOODS INVESTMENT COMPANY, P.O.BOX 870050, TECATE, CA 91987-0050.

41075

Redeemable at your local Adventist Book Center.
Not to be used in conjunction with any other offer.

Worthington, Natural Touch and Morningstar Farms are trademarks of Specialty Foods InvestmentCompany. TM, ® Specialty Foods Investment Company ©2002 Kellogg Company

5 28989 30076 3(8100)0 41075

$3.00 off — Manufacturer's Coupon — Expires 12/31/03 — $3.00 off

Save $3.00

on ONE CASE of Worthington® FriChik®

REGULAR OR LOW FAT

Worthington Foods Inc.

CONSUMER: OFFER IS LIMITED TO ONE COUPON PER CASE PURCHASED. COUPON MAY NOT BE REPRODUCED OR TRANSFERRED.
RETAILER: SPECIALTY FOODS INVESTMENT COMPANY will redeem this coupon in accordance with our redemption policy, copies available upon request. Cash value1/100¢. Void where prohibited, taxed, or restricted by law. Mail coupons to: KELLOGG COMPANY, P.O.BOX 870050, TECATE, CA 91987-0050.

41074

Redeemable at your local Adventist Book Center.
Not to be used in conjunction with any other offer.

Worthington is a trademark of Specialty Foods Investment Company. TM, ® Specialty Foods Investment Company ©2002 Kellogg Company

5 28989 52087 1(8100)0 41074

$3.00 off — Manufacturer's Coupon — Expires 12/31/03 — $3.00 off

Save $3.00

on ONE CASE of Loma Linda® Big Franks

REGULAR OR LOW FAT

Worthington Foods Inc.

CONSUMER: OFFER IS LIMITED TO ONE COUPON PER CASE PURCHASED. COUPON MAY NOT BE REPRODUCED OR TRANSFERRED.
RETAILER: SPECIALTY FOODS INVESTMENT COMPANY will redeem this coupon in accordance with our redemption policy, copies available upon request. Cash value1/100¢. Void where prohibited, taxed, or restricted by law. Mail coupons to: KELLOGG COMPANY, P.O.BOX 870050, TECATE, CA 91987-0050.

41073

Redeemable at your local Adventist Book Center.
Not to be used in conjunction with any other offer.

Worthington and Loma Linda are trademarks of Specialty Foods Investment Company. TM, ® Specialty Foods Investment Company ©2002 Kellogg Company

5 28989 74187 0(8100)0 41073

$3.00 off — Manufacturer's Coupon — Expires 12/31/03 — $3.00 off

Save $3.00

on ONE CASE of Worthington® FriPats®

Worthington Foods Inc.

CONSUMER: OFFER IS LIMITED TO ONE COUPON PER CASE PURCHASED. COUPON MAY NOT BE REPRODUCED OR TRANSFERRED.
RETAILER: SPECIALTY FOODS INVESTMENT COMPANY will redeem this coupon in accordance with our redemption policy, copies available upon request. Cash value1/100¢. Void where prohibited, taxed, or restricted by law. Mail coupons to: KELLOGG COMPANY, P.O.BOX 870050, TECATE, CA 91987-0050.

41072

Redeemable at your local Adventist Book Center.
Not to be used in conjunction with any other offer.

Worthington is a trademark of Specialty Foods Investment Company. TM, ® Specialty Foods Investment Company ©2002 Kellogg Company

5 28989 62087 8(8100)0 41072

$1.00 off — Manufacturer's Coupon — Expires 12/31/03 — $1.00 off

Save $1.00

on ONE JAR of Natural Touch® Kaffree Roma®

Worthington Foods Inc.

CONSUMER: OFFER IS LIMITED TO ONE COUPON PER JAR PURCHASED. COUPON MAY NOT BE REPRODUCED OR TRANSFERRED.
RETAILER: SPECIALTY FOODS INVESTMENT COMPANY will redeem this coupon in accordance with our redemption policy, copies available upon request. Cash value1/100¢. Void where prohibited, taxed, or restricted by law. Mail coupons to: SPECIALTY FOODS INVESTMENT COMPANY, P.O.BOX 870050, TECATE, CA 91987-0050.

41082

Redeemable at your local Adventist Book Center.
Not to be used in conjunction with any other offer.

Worthington and Natural Touch are trademarks of Specialty Foods Investment Company. TM, ® Specialty Foods Investment Company ©2002 Kellogg Company

5 28989 31176 9(8100)0 41082